BREAKING
DESTRUCTIVE
PATTERNS

Multiple Strategies for Treating Partner Abuse

Janet A. Geller

THE FREE PRESS
A Division of Macmillan, Inc.
NEW YORK

Maxwell Macmillan Canada
TORONTO

Maxwell Macmillan International
NEW YORK   OXFORD   SINGAPORE   SYDNEY

492

#25205377

The Free Press
A Division of Macmillan, Inc.
866 Third Avenue, New York, N.Y. 10022

Maxwell Macmillan Canada, Inc.
1200 Eglinton Avenue East
Suite 200
Don Mills, Ontario M3C 3N1

Macmillan, Inc. is part of the Maxwell Communication
Group of Companies.

Printed in the United States of America

printing number
1 2 3 4 5 6 7 8 9 10

Library of Congress Cataloging-in-Publication Data

Geller, Janet A.
    Breaking destructive patterns: multiple strategies for treating
    partner abuse / Janet A. Geller.
        p.   cm.
    Includes bibliographical references and index.
    ISBN 0–02–911605–8
    1. Abused wives—Counseling of—United States.   I. Title.
HV1445.G45   1992
362.82′92′0973—dc20   91-47754
                                                          CIP

*To Stan, who never once objected to
the time spent writing this book,
and who has been a constant support*

Contents

Preface

In my clinical experience working with battered women and batteries since 1976, I have observed that although all battered women have battering in common, not all of their needs are the same. With this awareness that abused women have diverse needs came the knowledge that no single method of intervention is applicable; rather, these women benefit from a multiplicity of approaches. This book describes an intervention model that uses multiple methods in the treatment of domestic violence. I hope that this book will provide practitioners several methods for intervening in cases of partner abuse.

I have drawn material concerning techniques and methodology primarily from my clinical experience, as well as the literature in the field. I had been considering such a book for a long time, but like others who practice a method of treatment, I was more absorbed in the doing than the telling. I believe that the telling can be useful to other practitioners in encouraging them to provide the treatment if they do not know how or to expand their knowledge if they are already engaged in some aspect of this practice.

The book is theoretical and descriptive, and it uses case examples extensively. It provides methods for treating battered women and batterers, individually and in groups and for working with the couples. Step-by-step descriptions for proceedings with treatment are included. I have made reference primarily to women being abused by men and, most often, wives by husbands; however, this book is intended for all instances where one adult partner is abusing the other adult partner, regardless of the relationship.

Chapter 1 describes the history of the treatment model and its rationale. Chapter 2 provides an overview of the problem of battered women, looking at it societally and psychologically. It examines as well the systems that battered women encounter.

When battered women are ready to leave the relationship, certain treatment approaches can reinforce and buttress their decision. Chapter 3 describes the use of treatment techniques that facilitate the client's decision to leave.

Chapter 4 describes the use of long-term support and survival skills training groups for women who wish to remain in the relationship. In chapter 5, the focus is on group treatment for batterers. Besides providing information on the development and implementation of the group, there is discussion on differential diagnosis concerning group suitability.

Chapter 6 deals with an innovative and radical approach to the treatment of battered women: conjoint therapy. It explains the rationale, suitability, and application of conjoint treatment.

Whether women remain or leave the battering relationship, they often get involved in the criminal justice and other systems. These systems are the subject of chapter 7.

Working with violence, particularly among family members, affects the practitioner's psyche in a powerful way. It is appropriate, therefore, to devote the last chapter to issues of countertransference and how to use it productively.

I thank Mary O'Donahue, bureau chief of the Child Abuse Unit at the District Attorney's Office, and Detective Lydia Martinez, domestic violence specialist in the New York City Police Department, for their invaluable and generous help with chapter 7 on the criminal justice system.

1

Introduction

B attered women's needs vary. Some women need to leave battering relationships; others wish to stay. Some benefit from support services while remaining at home; for others, a safe haven is imperative. Clearly, the various needs that battered women have require various treatment approaches. In other words, a multiplicity of interventions is needed. This book, directed to practitioners, presents a multimodality comprehensive model for the clinical treatment of battering, employing learning theory, interactive systemic thinking, and cognitive, behavioral, and communication techniques.

This book thus fills a gap in the domestic violence literature field. The voluminous literature existing about battering is focused primarily on research or description of the problem; only recently have treatment techniques begun to be described. This book is unique among treatment books in that it describes a multiple method of treatment rather than offers a singular focus.

I developed the model based on my experience of working with battered women as the clinical director of a women's center. Like every other women's center across the country, we were inundated with battered women in need of service, and like those in other such programs, the women we were serving did not want to leave their abusive partners, although they wanted the violence stopped.

Initially, like other women's centers, we counseled women to leave their abusive husbands and helped them strive to strike out on their own. We offered to guide clients through the court system so they could file and receive orders of protection, which would legally prohibit their husband's violent behavior, or so they could obtain

1

divorces. But for the most part, the women did not follow through this course offered by the criminal justice system, nor did they return to us for further assistance. Moreover, we discovered that only a very small percentage of battered women left or seriously intended to leave their battering partners.

In the 1970s, there were few counseling programs for battered women anywhere in the country. There were shelters and hot lines, but the women I saw, in the heart of suburban Suffolk County on eastern Long Island, New York, tended not to make use of the shelter system. The women tended to be migrants from the boroughs of New York City, fed up with urban conditions. They wanted a better way of life, with green lawns and safe streets for their children. These were traditional women; they believed in middle-class American values: the family, two cars in the garage, and a home that they owned formed the cornerstone of life. Their "gender pride and self-respect" demanded aspiring to family and parenthood and making a marriage work.[1] The women were primary caretakers and were proud that their husbands, the primary breadwinners, were able to provide them with this life in the suburbs. These were not women who were going to leave their husbands and move into a shelter, go on welfare, or take a low-paying job. It was clear that although they wanted the violence to stop, they were not going to break up their homes or the life-style they had aspired to achieve for so long. Most important, the women we came in contact with who proudly defined themselves as wives and mothers were not going to give up this role by leaving their homes. We learned all of this through paying close attention to what they were telling us and how they, not we, were defining their needs.

At the women's center, we tried to educate our clients to the position of members of the women's movement: that history and society have placed women in a deprived position subservient to men. We, too, believed, as feminists stated, that women and men are caught in sex role stereotyping that dictates how they play out their lives in American society, where women become the nurturers, feeling that the responsibility for the success of a relationship is theirs alone. Nevertheless, our attempts did not change our clients' desire to remain with their violent husbands. We then reevaluated the needs of clients and recognized that if they were not leaving their partners, another approach to the prevention and elimination of battering seemed to be called for. We reasoned that perhaps men could stop their violence.

A voluntary batterers' group aimed at the elimination of the violence seemed to make good sense. Not all batterers could benefit from such an intervention, but some would. The group was piloted, and it worked.[2] The men who came to the group, motivated by their desire to stop the violence, were people in pain too. Our initial negative view of these men was reshaped as a result of our work with them. Their violence, horrible and unacceptable as it was, was not their totality. Some of the men wanted to stop the violence. At the end of the short-term group (ten sessions), we decided to try to bring in their wives and run a couples group. Eliminating the violence was critical but not enough to restore the marriage, damaged from the abuse, to a healthy state.

The model thus developed began by working with the batterers to eliminate the violence. When we determined that the violence was no longer severe and the women were out of danger, we started treating the couples. These services were offered in addition to women's groups, batterers' groups, advocacy services, a hot line, and a shelter. The result was a comprehensive program offering a multiplicity of methods of intervention and alternatives to the clients.

My education and experience led to the model. As a social worker, I was taught the principle of beginning where the client is. Although this was in conflict with the women's movement position—that women do not make free choices about their societal sex roles and therefore society needs changing—we needed to address these clients, with their bruises, immediately. Moreover, the women were saying that they wanted to remain in their relationships, and the men were agreeing to come to us for help. My professional experience had prepared me for dealing with violence. I had worked with acting-out and aggressive populations in residential treatment centers for emotionally disturbed children and adolescents, inpatient psychiatric centers, poor populations in which violence was a part of daily life, and acting-out adolescents. The third facet of my background was that I was also trained as a family therapist and could apply the techniques used in family therapy to these couples.

In the remaining four years that I was at that center, the model was successfully employed. No formal research was conducted as to the model's effectiveness, rather, success was defined based on our experience. To date, outcome studies concerning the effectiveness of couples treatment has been very poor[3] although Margolin has documented its efficacy.[4]

In the intervening years, much has been written about the

dangers of treating couples. Some of the major criticisms are as follows: (1) Couples therapists focus in sessions on understanding the relationship of childhood influences and current functioning and ignore the violence. (2) Disclosure by women in the session is a cause for further abuse outside of the session. (3) Family systems therapists view violence systemically as a relationship issue, implying that there is equal responsibility for its occurrence and maintenance and that it serves a purpose in the relationship. The net result is blaming the victim, and minimizing the seriousness of the violence. Further, the fear of future violence inhibits women from speaking freely.[5] The warnings concerning the dangers of couples treatment are well heeded and must be taken into account. It is not necessary however, to abandon couples work if attention is given to taking appropriate measures to safeguard against the difficulties. When treating couples, the practitioner puts the emphasis on the batterer accepting total responsibility for the violence and addressing the need for the elimination of violence as the first order of business. Chapter 6 suggests an approach mindful of the above concerns.

I have continued to use this model. Although its basic form remains intact, I have learned from my clients and colleagues and modified it over time to fit current thinking about the needs of battered women. Seeing a couple separately until violence is under control, for example, is well accepted and employed in my model, as well as teaching about broader issues so both the battered women and their batterers understand the effects of gender development on their functioning and how they can change that if they wish. I am cognizant of the philosophy and thrust of the battered women's movement, which focuses on sociopolitical changes in a societal context; I am also aware of the battered women in my office who need something done now. It is in the interest of these battered women that I offer this model.

I hope that the information contained in this book, drawn from my experience of working with battered women for over nineteen years, will make a contribution to the field and increase practitioners' interest in helping a population so much in need. It is offered as one example of an approach to the effective treatment of battering. The chapters that follow explore the multiplicity of methods for addressing the needs of the battered women, tailoring treatment to each woman's individual needs. First, chapter 2 explores the world in which the battered woman lives.

2

Why Do They Stay?
Why Don't They Tell?

The Psychosocial Connection

In a representative sample using response analysis, a national probability survey of 2,143 couples revealed that in 1976, one of every twenty-six American wives (3.8 percent) is beaten by her husband, for the alarming total of almost 1.8 million annually.[1] Of female homicide victims, 30 percent are killed by their husbands or boyfriends, and a woman is beaten every 15 seconds in the United States.[2] More recent data on the incidence of battering indicate that between 12 million and 15 million women in the United States have been physically abused at least once by their male partners.[3] In New York City alone in 1987, there were 200,245 family dispute calls, many of them concerning wife battering.[4] The above 30 percent female homicide victims killed by husbands or boyfriends is a conservative estimate obtained from police statistics. Most women do not report the batterings to the police or, for that matter, to their doctors, their social workers, or anyone else. In one survey, of 109 women who reported a total of 32,000 assaults during their marriages, 517 (less than 2 percent) were reported to the police.[5]

Mental health providers and physicians may see and treat battered women but generally not for family violence. Elaine Hilberman, a psychiatrist notes that a large percentage of women being treated for depression, eating and sleeping disorders, emotional lability, and anxiety are actually victims of family violence, although these women typically do not reveal information about their battering. She also

5

found a strong correlation between physical abuse and subsequent suicide or murder.[6] According to one practitioner most obstetrician-gynecologists have patients who are victims of battering, although the women do not acknowledge the abuse. This physician has found battering to be the major cause of injury to women, with one-quarter to one-half of all emergency room visits by women a result of battering.[7]

Although more than ever before people who are experiencing family violence are making this fact known, silence is still the more common response. The case of seven-year-old Lisa Steinberg, who died at the hands of her adult charges who beat her, graphically portrays the silence that most battered women exhibit. The major focus of this case was on child abuse, but another form of abuse existed in that family as well. Hedda Nussbaum, the woman who raised Lisa, had been a battered woman for many years. She did not reveal the extent of the batterings until the terrible tragedy of Lisa became known. An excerpt from her testimony where the abuse to her was revealed illustrates this point:

Q: Miss Nussbaum, did there come a time that Mr. Steinberg began to complain about you?

A: Yes . . .

Q: Did there come an escalation from just verbally complaining about you?

A: Yes.

Q: What was the next step?

A: He struck me . . .

Q: What was your reaction?

A: I was very surprised, and I thought it would never happen again.

Q: Did there come a time when it did happen again?

A: Yes . . .

Q: Now, Miss Nussbaum, directing your attention to the end of 1983, the early part of 1984, what was your relationship with Mr. Steinberg like at that period of time?

A: At that time he began beating me severely.[8]

Commonly, battered women remain silent and stay in their abusive relationships. Why they do will be better understood by exploring the battered woman's world. This chapter discusses society's attitudes about battered women, the myths surrounding battered women that blame the victim, the more subtle psychological under-currents concerning society's views of victims, and the systems that reinforce the status quo (the clergy, the social service and criminal justice systems, and the medical profession).

THE VIEW FROM THE OUTSIDE: FORCES AGAINST CHANGE

Battering has been referred to as a conspiracy of silence. The conspirators are the battered women themselves, the batterers, their children and other relatives, and the systems with which battered women come into contact. Why battered women remain silent has complex origins encompassing society's values and attitudes, myths about battered women, how the systems with which battered women interface negatively affect them, and economic considerations.

The Societal Context

Society's Values

Although less so today than previously, the sanctity of the family has been a hallmark of American life. The American dream encompasses the happy and wholesome American family, where "a man's home is his castle." Women beaten inside those homes did not fit in with this American vision of home and hearth, captured in such classic television shows as "Ozzie and Harriet" and "Father Knows Best." Knowledge that women were being beaten by their partners disturbed America's view of families as the cornerstone of American life and the notion of romantic love whose bottom-line message is that love conquers all.[9]

Society's Attitudes

Society basically views battered women unsympathetically. Adults, it is believed, make their own choices. A woman who is abused yet remains in the relationship is making a free choice. In effect, the woman is blamed for living in an abusive relationship.

Martin Symonds, a psychiatrist, has proposed several reasons for society's attitudes toward the victim. First, if she were not at fault for her partner's abuse, then any woman could be beaten. But if blame can be cast, those who feel they have done nothing to provoke battering can feel safe that they will not find themselves victims of violence. The result is to blame the battered woman for the abuse. Second, there is an unconscious fear of contamination by association, so society isolates the victim. Yet another reason arises from a definition of a victim as a living being selected for sacrifice to keep the rest of the community free from harm. Further, according to the Judeo-Christian heritage, we believe in reaping what we sow—or you get what you deserve. Finally, society believes in personal control and asks the victim, "Couldn't you tell? Why did you stay?"[10]

Myths

There are numerous myths about battered women: battering occurs only in a certain segment of the population; she "deserved" it because she was so provocative; she got beaten because she could not manage her man; if she wanted to leave, she would; anyone who lets a man beat her deserves it.

The Interfacing Systems

Psychiatric Community

Compounding the prevalent blaming-the-victim mentality is the condemnation by the psychiatric community, which attaches psychological labels to battered women. A psychiatrist might say that a victim has a "masochistic personality disorder" or that the couple has a "sadomasochistic relationship." Battered women are more likely than nonbattered women to be diagnosed with a pseudo-psychiatric label, such as "hysteria" or "neurotic." It is not uncommon for them ultimately to be institutionalized in mental hospitals.[11]

In my experience of training mental health professionals, inevitably the question of a battered woman's pathology arises, with trainees consistently desirous of giving her a psychiatric diagnosis. "Battered woman syndrome" explains the psychological changes these women undergo over time. The term is free from the stigma of viewing these women pathologically, but it is not accepted by the psychiatric community as an official diagnosis; rather, it is a subcategory of post-traumatic stress disorder.[12]

Criminal Justice System

Police who respond to a woman's call for help may find the crime is over by the time they arrive. Sometimes the batterer has fled, and there is nothing for the authorities to do. The battered woman may get the impression that the police do not care.[13] Sometimes the battered woman and batterer turn against the police when they arrive; the highest rate of police mortality occurs at the scene of domestic disputes.

Until 1977 in New York City, battering was a family court, not a criminal court, matter. The role of the family court was to mediate, not punish.* Although today the police response in New York City is somewhat better as a result of a class action suit filed by battered women against the Police Department and the persistence of battered women advocates, women and advocates report that many officers nevertheless do not treat battering seriously or accurately inform women of their rights under the law. Laws protecting battered women remain weak and ineffective, and the court system is encumbered. Women are not educated about their legal rights or how to make effective use of the criminal justice system, weak as it may be. (Chapter 7 elaborates on the problem and suggests some solutions.)

Medical System

More than 1 million battered women see physicians each year, but many well-meaning doctors do not know how to address the problem adequately, and many do not address it at all.[14] Some will accept a woman's excuse that she received her bruises as a result of a fall down the stairs, and some question her in a manner that results in her feeling further victimized. If women are not discouraged by the reactions and attitudes of medical personnel, they are often repelled and disheartened if they have to wait for hours to be seen in the emergency room.[15]

Clergy

Women who confide in the clergy do not always find a helpful response. They may be advised to stay in the home for the child-

*Laws regarding what type of an offense battering is considered vary from state to state, with some states having stricter penalties than others.

ren's sake, to try to be a better wife, and to learn to endure, with reward coming in the next life. A survey of Protestant ministers found a patriarchal attitude toward women they counseled. Twenty-one percent felt that no amount of abuse would justify a wife's leaving her husband. The majority would justify separation only if the abuse was severe. Severe usually means serious injury, the woman's life is in danger, or abuse with a weapon. Twenty-six percent agreed with the statement, "A wife should submit to her husband and trust that God would honor her action by either stopping the abuse or giving her the strength to endure it."[16] Traditionally, clergy are opposed to families' breaking up and therefore may not counsel what may be in the best interests of a battered woman.

Social Service and Mental Health System

Women who seek help from the social services or mental health system for depression, substance abuse, emotional lability, eating and sleeping disorders, somatic complaints and vague ailments, irritability, nervousness, and even marital and relationship problems may have as their root cause that they are being battered.[17] But battering often remains an underlying problem that never surfaces because battered women rarely reveal their abuse unless questioned directly. Most social services and mental health agencies do not routinely ask about domestic violence as part of their intake procedure or in counseling sessions. The number of agencies providing services to battered women is small in proportion to the problem, and most provide no services at all—a lack clearly revealed by these agencies' advertisements, which are silent about services for battered women. And it appears from the responses I receive in my own practice that private practitioners who treat battering follow the same pattern as social agencies and mental health services.

A recent case at which I testified illustrates this lack of attention. The woman involved, a nurse married to a lawyer prominent in his community, had never revealed to her psychiatrist of several years that she was a battered woman. Only during the ending phase of her treatment did she tell him. The psychiatrist had suspected something of this nature but had never asked. Perhaps he considered it good practice to wait until the client was able to tell rather than probe.

She, on the other hand, may have interpreted his response (or lack of one) as a message to remain silent.

A simple solution is to ask about battering on the client intake form or for workers to address it early in treatment. But agreeing to treat battered women is not enough. These clients need nontraditional services that facilitate immediate intervention. Most agencies and clinics are not designed to provide this kind of help. This book addresses the lack of specialization to battered women in social services agencies, in mental health clinics, and with private practitioners by providing suggested treatment approaches that existing services can adapt.

Substance Abuse and Partner Abuse

The relationship of substance abuse to partner abuse is beginning to receive attention. No causal relationship exists; that is, substance abuse does not cause partner abuse, but in many cases where domestic violence is present, substance abuse is also present.[18] There is another facet to substance abuse here: the relationship between battered women and substance abuse.

Physicians not uncommonly prescribe tranquilizers or sleeping pills for their patients.[19] If a woman reveals she is being battered, the physician may prescribe medication to calm her or help her sleep. Women who complain of irritability, depression, or lability, for example, but make no mention of abuse may be offered the same solution. The effect is that many women become addicted to pills as a way of coping with violence.

Battered women may turn to alcohol and drug abuse after the onset of violence.[20] Sometimes they use substances to escape emotionally from the realities of their situation, or they join their partners in abusing substances to avoid yet another reason for his abusing her (for example, she refuses to drink or pop pills with him). For some men, substance usage mellows them, giving their partners motive for encouraging their substance abuse.

Employers

For certain women who are battered, work provides a welcome escape. They can feel productive, effective, and useful; in other words, work can be empowering. One client whose self-esteem, typically, had eroded with being abused brightened when talking about herself at work, saying, "Everybody likes me." This was the one area in her life where she did not feel herself a failure. But for other women, their functioning at work decreases as a result of the violence in their lives.

Although a number of businesses provide employee assistance programs, designed to help, and thereby retain, good workers who are suffering from personal problems, including domestic violence, the bottom line in the workplace is production. Employers cannot afford to tolerate the limitlessly decreased production of a woman who comes to work late regularly because her husband woke her up at 3:00 A.M. and abused her and she could not get up on time, or he injured her so badly that she could not get up at all or appear on the job with her bruises evident. Eventually, Hedda Nussbaum voluntarily quit her job at Random House because of Joel Steinberg's violence. Nor will they tolerate for long a woman who needs to make numerous telephone calls at work that she cannot make at home, an angry partner who harasses her at work, or violent men who show up at the worksite. Eventually she is let go; at best, she is tolerated but stigmatized.

Economic Factors

Economically women are driven back to their abusing situation because of unsatisfactory and limited resources. Leaving a battering partner usually means a reduced life-style because of a lowered income. An employed woman has to adjust to living on one income instead of two. A nonemployed woman has to become employable or go on welfare.

I am reminded of one courageous woman with whom I worked. Her husband earned a good living, she had three beautiful children, she had plenty to be proud of, and she enjoyed her role as homemaker and primary caretaker. She was also battered by her substance-abusing husband, who earned enough money to buy drugs and maintain a nice home.

My client came to see me after the school called her in because one of her children was acting out. What began as family therapeutic sessions quickly turned into sessions to help her leave her husband; he was unreachable and not interested in change. She eventually did leave. She was unable to use a shelter because she owned a house in another part of the country, left to her in her mother's will, and did not want a lien put on it to make her financially eligible for shelter aid. She moved from a spacious five-room apartment in a nice section of New York City to an apartment in a city project with fewer rooms and in a poor neighborhood. Because she had no job skills and was not a high school graduate, she took her general equivalency diploma and entered a training program. When she finishes, the highest salary she can earn will be far less than what her husband earned, and she will have to juggle career and motherhood. Currently, she is working two days a week (one of them Saturday) in the only job she could find. She can no longer afford to dress the children or herself the way she used to or spend money as she used to. Her husband wants her back.

When battered women look to society for help, they have few places to turn, and most resources are ineffective and limited. Stark and Flitcraft note, "Institutional maltreatment plays a critical role in battering as well. As help is either denied or actually turned against the abused woman, her options are closed, she feels entrapped, and may become alternately passive or hostile."[21] Society blames her, the systems often do not help her or, worse, they harm her, and the specialized services available are limited and inadequate. That is the view from the outside—externally. In view of the realities, why women remain silent and why they stay in battering relationships becomes understandable. The view from the inside—the psychological face—further supports why change is so difficult and how psychological forces act to maintain the status quo.

THE VIEW FROM THE INSIDE

In addition to the societal attitudes against women living with violence and the counterproductive effects of interfacing systems, women themselves, paradoxically, tend to hold these same attitudes as well. They, too, are members of society.

The Paralytic Effects of Socialization

Susan Brownmiller has described the structures of Western civilization that account for treating women as possessions, giving men the right to dominate and abuse them.[22] According to this perspective, male domination over women is pervasive and embedded in the culture; both men and women sanction and accept it. Husbands exert power and control over their wives, and violence perpetrated against women is considered acceptable. For example, part of English Common Law, upon which our laws are based, the "rule of thumb" law gave husbands the right to beat their wives with a stick, provided it was no thicker than the size of his thumb. Straus and Hotaling have also noted that violence in the family, such as physical discipline of children, and victimization against women, have been legitimized.[23] Superimposed on the acceptance of violence in the family is the sanction of societal violence, such as wars, development and use of defense weapons, and capital punishment, "for the good of society."[24] Additionally, socialization theory posits that gender formation results in prescribed gender roles by which males dominate and females submit and nurture. With all of these influences combined, it is not surprising that many men are violent toward women and that there is little protest about this situation. Women who are being abused not uncommonly remain silent and accepting of the situation.

One client told of her anger at her women friends because they never talked about their husbands' beating them as hers did. It never occurred to her they were not talking of beatings because their husbands did not beat them. She accepted it as a fact of life that husbands beat their wives.

Psychological Determinants

Leonore Walker, in describing the battered woman syndrome, and Martin Symonds, in discussing stages of victimization, cogently present the psychological factors that contribute to the reasons that women do not leave their battering situation. Symonds's theory and Walker's explanation of learned helplessness also help to explain why battered women remain silent.

Walker has written volumes about the battered women syndrome. It is beyond the scope of this book to present her theory in its entirety. Basically, according to Walker, the battered woman syndrome and the theory of learned helplessness, when viewed together, help us to understand what happens to battered women psychologically. She points out that the effects of post-traumatic stress disorder, of which the battered woman syndrome is a subcategory, are that certain psychological symptoms develop in most people that continue to affect their functioning, even long past the original trauma. One of the symptoms might be the belief that they are helpless to change their situation. Continuous and unpredictable traumatic events such as battering can result in the development of coping mechanisms to deal with the trauma rather than developing strategies to escape the traumatic situation because of the belief, real or perceived, that nothing they or anyone can do will change their situation. The belief that they cannot change their situation develops as a result of women learning from experience that they cannot predict the effect their behavior will have on the batterer and/or that actual defense is impossible. In order to minimize harm, then, various coping skills are employed with women more likely to choose behaviors that will result in known and/or familiar outcomes having a high probability of protecting them, rather than responses that result in an unknown outcome, like escape.[25] Walker states that women initially attempt to influence the batterer's violent behavior but eventually learn that they are powerless in the face of the assaults. No matter what they do, the violence does not cease. Instead there is a three-phase cyclical pattern, which Walker labels the cycle of violence.

In phase one, the tension-building phase, minor battering incidents occur where the woman feels she has some influence on the situation. She tries to keep things calm by being docile, which can result in an escalation of violence because the batterer can misinterpret her calmness as proof that he can abuse her. The cycle usually progresses, her influence lessens, and his violence increases to the acute phase, which is phase two. In the acute phase, the violence has become vicious and severe and she has no control. When the violence erupts or stops is unpredictable and decided upon by the batterer. The woman often feels psychologically trapped. Phase two is followed by a period of remorse and reconciliation. During the remorse stage, the partners' love is rekindled, giving women the false hope that the violence will stop and the relationship will improve.[26] In behavioral theory, this is called intermittent reinforcement, and it has proved to be more effective than either positive or negative reinforcement. In intermittent reinforcement, sometimes there is positive reward and other times not.[27] During the period of remorse, the woman receives what is akin to positive reinforcement; once the cycle begins again, negative reinforcement replaces positive reinforcement, until the next period of remorse, and so on. Women get hooked into waiting for a return of remorse, with the accompanied positive response from their partners.

Symonds's construct concerning crime victims' responses corresponds to my view of the battered woman syndrome. Exhibit 2–1 shows how certain aspects of Symond's theory can apply to what I have observed about victims of battering. Initially, according to Symonds, victims display shock, denial, and disbelief. During the beginning stages of abuse, strong defense mechanisms are at work. The woman minimizes, rationalizes, and externalizes the violence, denying that it is serious. Her partner joins with the same defenses. At this time, neither party believes violence has become a major focal point in their lives. This is the stage of excuses.

The next stage of Symonds's theory of victimization is fear— either fighting fear or frozen fear. In fighting fear, the person fights back. Some battered women do fight back by taking legal measures, leaving their partners, or physically fighting back. One women who was obese told me that she had never before been overweight; she gained weight in order to be an equal match with her abusing husband in physical fights. Some women who fight back, however, find themselves in a different kind of difficulty. A woman who seriously injuries her batterer in the process and it is not self-defense can be incarcerated.* Further, many women who initially fight back physically often stop because their partners are stronger. Instead, most women respond to violence with frozen fear: they do nothing. This is partially a gender issue, for women are taught to be submissive and nonassertive, and partially due to immobilized fear and the belief that there is no recourse.

Symonds refers to psychological infantilism, or clinging behavior, as another response to victimization. This response frequently occurs in hostage crises. In a hostage situation, victims depend on their captors to keep them alive and, ironically, become grateful to them. Sometimes they identify with their captors and become hostile to the authorities upon the aggressors' capture. I have found that battered women feel that they owe their lives to their violent partners because the men could have killed them in their violence and did not. They feel grateful and depend on their partners to keep them alive.

*In general, women are not as physically powerful as men. They often plan retaliation rather than fighting back during a battering, which would be self-defense. In contrast, a planned retaliation is considered premeditated, and premeditated crimes are punishable. In the television movie "The Burning Bed," the woman planned the murder of her abusive husband; she waited for him to go to sleep and then set fire to him in bed, burning him to death.

Exhibit 2–1 *Symonds Theory of Victimization Applied to Battered Women*

Theory of Victimology	Battered Women
Shock, denial, disbelief	Displays strong defense mechanisms Minimizes violence Uses excuses
Fear: Fighting or frozen	Fights back or displays helplessness and apathy
Psychological infantilism, clinging behavior	Shows gratitude and dependency Identifies with the aggressor
Self-recrimination	Blames self, as does the batterer
Rage: Outward or inward	Directs rage to batterer (outward) Becomes depressed and apathetic, stifles anger (inward)
Loss	Loses faith in society's values on the family Loses faith in love and marriage Loses confidence Loses husband they married

Victims, according to Symonds, feel self-recrimination or blame; they believe their victimization was their fault. Battered women blame themselves for the abuse for several reasons: as nurturers, they believe they are responsible for what happens in the home; their partners blame them, and they accept the blame; and, paradoxically, to be at fault is a way of being powerful. If something is one's fault, one can change it by finding the right thing to do.

Symonds talks about rage as a response to victimization. It can be directed outward, at the abuser, helping the woman to take action, but more typically it is misdirected onto the women themselves. Rage directed inward results in depression and apathy. One author comments that battered women stifle their anger for fear of the rage that would be unleashed if they allowed themselves to be in touch with their anger.[28]

Loss is another response that Symonds identifies. Battered women lose faith in society's values concerning the meaning of family and faith in love and marriage, confidence in themselves, and the husband they thought they had.

Battered women face a multitude of obstacles to change. In

essence, the questions frequently asked concerning why they remain silent and why they stay were addressed in this chapter by the glimpse into their internal and external worlds. Without an understanding of the lives of these women, it is hard to treat them effectively.

This background information puts battered women in context. Although most battered women experience some or all of the factors described, each woman has an individual response to the violence, and therefore differential treatment may be called for. A repertoire of treatment interventions as opposed to a singular intervention best serves the different needs of battered women and helps practitioners to reach a wider range of women.

3

Leaving

The Use of Transitional Counseling

Estimates are that 3 million to 4 million women in the United States are battered,[1] yet only a small percentage of them—perhaps less than 10 percent—end their relationship with the abuser. When these women are ready to leave, certain treatment approaches can reinforce and buttress their decision. This chapter describes the use of treatment techniques that will facilitate the client's decision to leave in nonemergency situations and help her to stay away once she does leave. The techniques, chosen from my multimodality approach for women planning to leave, combine the development of a safety plan, strategies for living as a single person, knowledge of community resources, case management, and supportive counseling. Women who have not yet left their partners need to be taught survival skills. After they leave, therapy might be important to them, either individually or in a group.

EMERGENCY LEAVING

Emergencies require an immediate response to ensure that the woman is out of danger. A woman should leave her home when:

1. There is imminent danger—for example, the batterer is threatening to harm her, and she is afraid that he will.
2. Any woman who states a desire to leave should be helped to do so and lastly,
3. The home is not safe in the worker's judgment. Battered

19

woman numb themselves to the abuse as a means of survival
and may not be fully aware of imminent danger. In such a case,
the worker may suggest she leave. The final decision is the
woman's, but the worker can be directive by suggesting she
leave, stating the reasons for the suggestion, including the
worker's opinion that she is not safe at home, and working
through reluctance about leaving.

Holly came into the office as a walk-in. She had two black eyes, a
cut on her forehead, a jaw that was beginning to swell, and
bruises on her body. Her hair was in disarray and her clothes
torn and bloody. Tears were streaming down her face. Her
husband had just beaten her, and she was shaking. I asked if she
would like something warm to drink—a cup of tea or broth. She
nodded her head. I asked what had happened, and she told me.
I told her I was glad she had come here, and I would help her.
When I told her I was glad she was alive, more tears streamed
down her face, and she began to sob softly. I waited. I asked
where she hurt and discussed getting medical attention. She did
not know if she wanted to see a doctor; indeed, she did not
know what she wanted to do. I told her there were various
options open to her and explained the possibilities.

After awhile, Holly sighed. I asked if she felt a little calmer
now. A small, tentative smile crossed her face as she looked at
me, nodding, and she said, "A little." I asked what she was
going to do when she left here. She shrugged and said, "Go
home." I asked where her husband was. She guessed he was at
home. I wondered if she thought she would be safe or whether
he would start beating her again. She said, blankly, that she did
not know. I questioned her about his past patterns. She replied
that sometimes he would start again, and sometimes he would
not. She did not know what to expect.

Her beating seemed severe to me, and she seemed traumatized. When I told her I thought she might want to stay
somewhere else tonight, she protested vigorously. I asked why
not, and she replied that she just wanted to go home and get
some rest. I agreed that she needed rest but wondered if she
would be able to get that at home. She did not know. The blank
look returned to her face. I explained the reasons I thought she
should consider leaving tonight: she said that her husband

might get violent again, she was badly beaten, and she should not run the risk of further injury. She said that she needed quiet time to recover and heal. I told her there were various places she could go other than home, describing what they were like and that there would be people to help her and other women like herself to talk to. I also mentioned motels and hotels, friends and family. She was hesitant: "I—I don't know." I told her my opinion was that she should leave, although I would respect any decision she made. Perhaps she should take some time to decide.

Holly, I believe, was suffering from trauma and not thinking clearly. I thought she was minimizing the danger at home and thought that she could get hit again. For these reasons, I took a strong position in favor of an alternative place to stay.

The worker is responsible for finding a resource for women who opt for emergency shelter: a shelter, hotel or motel for a woman with financial resources or friends and family. In these situations, family tend to be underutilized. Many women say that they cannot turn to family when perhaps they can. The worker should carefully explore this possibility because the support of family members is important help. Family care in a crisis reinforces a natural bond that is emotionally uplifting; its significance should not be overlooked.

If there is the possibility of the woman's being cared for by family members, the woman can call from the worker's office and make the arrangements. If the woman would like her family to come to her aid but does not think they will, a reluctant family member might be receptive to the worker's intervention. In this case, the worker places the call in the presence of the woman. She identifies herself, tells the family member that her relative is in grave danger from her husband who beats her, and says that she needs the family member to protect and take care of her.

Battered women can locate services in their relatives' communities through the national toll-free hot line that lists such resources nationwide: 1-800-333-SAFE.

In an emergency, the worker's role is to provide immediate intervention concerning the women's safety and well-being. When there is no emergency, contact will be longer term, and there is an extended time to think through decisions.

NONEMERGENCY LEAVE TAKING

Jackie had two beautiful children she deeply cared about. She was very proud of how good looking they were and poured much time and energy into their appearance. Her husband earned a good salary, which she lavished on the children by buying clothes. Not only were they beautiful; they were nice children too; everyone told her so. One day, Jackie got a call from the school reporting that her 11-year-old son was becoming a behavioral problem. An alarmed Jackie rushed to school. She told the guidance counselor that she thought her son might be upset over the home situation. She and her husband fought a lot (she emphasized *a lot*). The counselor asked if the fights got out of hand, Jackie held her head down and nodded. The counselor asked if there was ever any violence; Jackie nodded again. The counselor gently asked if Jackie wanted some help for herself, commenting that it looked as if she needed someone to talk to. Jackie resisted; she had stood this a long time and did not need anything for herself. The counselor pointed out that Jackie thought that her son might be upset over the fights and that her going for help would help him too. The counselor knew there was another child and said that she imagined her daughter must be upset also at seeing her mother getting hit. She asked Jackie if her daughter was showing any signs of being troubled. When Jackie said no, the counselor replied, "You mean, 'Not yet.'" Jackie's concern over her children prompted her to call me for help. She thought she wanted to be seen alone first and then maybe with her children. She talked about getting out of her home.

It is not uncommon for women initially to think in terms of ending the relationship when they call for help. Typically something has precipitated the call; for Jackie, it was the concern for her children. But although women may state that they want to get out, they may change their minds. Experience and the literature support the notion that few women actually leave. A battered woman who changes her mind should not be problematic for the worker; she or he simply charts new directions. But the situation might prove problematic for the woman because she may believe she has contracted with the worker to leave. She may not know that she can change her mind, that there are other options, and that she may continue counseling. Additionally, shame, fear, or guilt may deter her from continuing counseling.

After she has told the worker the reasons she wants to leave, typically describing the violence she has endured, and the worker and she join in this effort to help her to get out, she might be ashamed to admit a change of mind.

With the worker and she investing their energies in preparing her to leave, she might be afraid there is no turning back. She might even fear that the worker will be angry at her for changing her mind. Let us keep in mind that battered women are used to responses of anger when they have displeased their husband. Batterers often threaten the women with bodily harm if she leaves, promising revenge on her and her family members. These threats can be enough to cause her to stay.

Finally, realizing the efforts the worker has made to find her resources, the woman might feel guilty about putting the worker through trouble for nothing. She might find it easier to end treatment rather than admit to the worker that she changed her mind and has decided to stay in the home.

Once the woman leaves treatment, she cannot be helped. When a woman is able to overcome great odds and take the step toward help, the worker must make every effort not to lose her from the treatment process. To ensure against her dropping out of counseling should she decide to stay in the relationship, all of her options should be laid out, as I did with Claudia.

Claudia called telling me that she was married to an abusive man and was finally ready to leave but did not know where to turn or what to do. She wanted help in drawing up a plan of action. I said I would be happy to help her with that. Before I could continue, she interrupted saying she had tried that once before, but her husband had pleaded and begged, promising to change. He had, briefly, but had started abusing her again. She claimed she would never fall for that a second time; she wanted out. I told her that she certainly seemed determined, but I could help her with other options too. Whatever help she wanted, I would give her. We could switch direction at any time. I outlined the options, but she said she was sure she wanted to leave. I suggested that we work on that.

In our first meeting, Claudia was firm about leaving, but at the end of the session, she told me she was worried about her son, who was very close to his father. She asked me to tell her again about her other options. At the third session, Claudia sheepishly wondered if leaving was the best solution. Now that she had an order of protection,* her husband was nervous about her calling the police and she thought he would not hit her so readily. When he was not abusive to her, he "wasn't such a bad guy." She thought maybe he should go to group counseling. I told her again about the batterers' group we ran.

The next session, Claudia again wanted to leave. Her friends had reminded her of his abusiveness and told her she was "crazy" to stay. She thought maybe she should leave temporarily. If he went to the group and stopped his violence, maybe she would return. I suggested that we continue working on her plan to leave.

Claudia vacillated for some time before she arrived at a decision with which she was truly comfortable. She was able to return to the sessions because she knew that I would offer her whatever available service she wanted. She felt the freedom to use the sessions to explore her options thoroughly. Contrast this example, where options were kept open, to the following one, from the early days of a program of which I was the clinical director. There, our efforts were more narrowly concentrated on helping women to leave.

Our hot-line telephone was constantly busy with women calling who were battered. We told them about their legal rights: that they could have their husbands arrested, they could get orders of protection, and so forth. We told them that they could leave the relationship and informed them about shelters where they would be safe and about separation or divorce from their violent partners. We helped them work out strategies and action plans, both on the hot line and in the counseling center. The women received our initial suggestions with enthusiasm, but after a session or two, we did not hear from them again. We were puzzled, baffled, and frustrated, and we found that we were not alone. Our colleagues had experienced the same results, concluding that this was the nature of the problem;

---

*An order of protection is a court order prohibiting the defendant from behaving in certain harmful ways, like battering, verbal abuse, etc. If violated, it could result in a jail sentence.

battered women called in a crisis and stopped calling when the crisis was over, calling again in the next crisis.

This situation did not sit well with me. I decided to call back a woman who had dropped out and hear directly from her why she did so. It was a risk to call her because her husband might have answered the telephone, possibly putting her in danger, and, since she stopped calling us, I did not want to intrude upon her privacy. Nevertheless, after much discussion, it was decided that I would make the call. If her husband answered, I would ask for someone else, pretending to have the wrong number. I was in luck: she answered the telephone and was willing and able to talk. I explained that I wanted to understand why she had stopped her contact with the worker; her answers could help us to improve our services. I made it clear that I was in no way trying to convince her to see us again. She responded that she found us to be very good; the worker was helpful and nice; she had no complaints whatsoever. However, when she changed her mind and decided not to create an adversarial relationship with her husband, she did not have the "heart to disappoint the worker" who had worked so hard for her, free of charge.

This woman's response taught us an important lesson: although all battered women have battering in common, not all of them benefit from the same approach. Through our experience with this woman and hundreds of others, we changed our approach concerning how we presented the option to leave, which includes giving women permission to change their mind. When it is clear that a woman does want to leave, strategies need to be developed to help her carry through on this decision. She needs to sustain herself against the powerful pull to go back, which is very common.[2]

WHEN WOMEN WANT TO LEAVE

Women in a nonemergency situation have the luxury of planning ahead; they will not be leaving immediately but over time. For them the focus is on developing strategies for leaving. They need a safety plan, information and referral, financial planning, case management, and supportive counseling.

Initially she and the worker develop a plan in preparation for leaving sometime in the future, when the leave-taking plan is complete. This plan develops both short- and long-term goals.

The Safety Plan

Short-term goals focus on the woman's immediate needs: safety and coexistence with the batterer. Since she continues to live with the batterer in this planning phase, an individualized safety plan tailored to her situation is critical. For some women, it might be necessary to go to the police and secure an order of protection. For other women, using the criminal justice system might arouse suspicion and unnecessarily anger the batterer; in this case, another means of being safe must be developed. A woman who came to see me fell into the second category. She believed that any legal involvement would arouse her partner's suspicion. A lawyer had encouraged her to get an order of protection, and although she had completed the tedious process, she decided not to serve the papers. Instead, she developed a plan for visiting a "sick relative" for several days, which gave her time to plan further and time away from him. When she returned from visiting her "sick relative," we made another arrangement for her to leave should she notice signs of violence.

The safety plan lays out steps to take to be safe and includes heightening the woman's awareness of signs of impending violence so that she can avoid or deescalate the situation before it reaches an explosion. She may also be able to escape when she notes signals indicating escalating anger. (In chapter 4, the section "Teaching of Survival Skills Strategies" describes how to notice signs of violence.) Her safety plan is written down, and the worker keeps a copy. She may or may not be given a copy; the decision depends on whether she can safely have it in her possession. Some batterers rummage through women's belongings for signs of disloyalty. While she is waiting to leave, it is important not to arouse her partner's suspicions and to live with him as peacefully as possible. This is what happened in the case of Shirelle.

Shirelle wanted out. There was no emergency; she wanted to take the time to map out an effective plan and have everything in place before she left. When I asked how easy it would be for her to remain with her husband, she felt she could "manage" him. I thought we should develop a safety plan nonetheless, just in case she needed one. She did not want to take any legal action as she was certain it would make for a more adversarial relationship. She had friends and parents she could go to should she need to get away. Her friends knew her situation and were supportive.

We discussed ways to keep calm at home in the meantime. I asked her if her husband gave signals of escalating violence. At first she said she did not know. Sometimes they argued and it did not lead to violence, and other times it did. I asked if there was a difference between the two. She said, "Wait a minute. Come to think of it, he curses a lot before he's angry enough to get violent." We agreed that this was the signal. At the sign of excessive cursing, she should avoid him or leave the house. I wrote this all down, step by step. I asked if it was safe for her to have a copy, which it was.

Information and Referral

A battered woman usually needs a lawyer who is familiar with domestic abuse; the potential for violence may require a different approach concerning separation and divorce than in other such cases. Lawyers unfamiliar with partner abuse often do not fully comprehend the volatility of the woman's situation. Practitioners should acquire a list of lawyers women have had good experiences with and inform the client about her legal rights. Other referrals might include housing, job training, and community resources.

Financial Planning

Women who have time to plan leaving may be able to place themselves in a more advantageous financial position. Where possible, she can open her own savings account in her name and in a different bank from her partner, for two reasons: to establish her own financial credibility and to avoid her partner's discovering her account. Possibly she can establish a checking account in her name also. Any credit cards should be put in her name so she has access to credit when she leaves. She may need to charge items or take a cash advance. Probably, however, her partner will cancel the cards when she leaves. Another option is to get a credit card in her name. Most services she will need to avail herself of prefer to deal with credit cards, and it is a sure way of establishing creditworthiness. Any property and/or possessions can be in her name as well as his.

Certain states have common property laws; in the event of a divorce, each partner automatically gets half.

A woman's freedom is more limited although not impossible without monetary means. For women without access to financial resources, the local department of social services can provide financial assistance. Women need to be instructed in how to apply for financial aid and how to deal effectively with this system, which varies from locality to locality. Workers who are knowledgeable about negotiating the social welfare system can provide valuable help.

There are other financial avenues as well. Can she get a loan? Borrow from someone? Although some of the possibilities may seem unlikely, the questions should be asked, because sometimes uncommon possibilities arise.

Case Management

Case management is the systematic process of assessment, planning, service coordination and referral, and monitoring through which the multiple service needs of battered women are met. By providing information, referral, and help in financial planning, the worker fulfills the case management role. The case management plan may warrant changing as the woman's situation unfolds over time.

Supportive Counseling

Supportive counseling is ongoing. Extricating themselves completely from abusive relationships is extremely difficult for battered women. They need reassurance, affirmation of their courage, help with their fears, and reminders of why they are leaving.

As a woman gains emotional distance from her partner and she is successfully avoiding contact with him when he is angry, one of two things is likely to happen: her commitment to leave becomes reinforced, or she forgets how bad the situation was. For some women, the lessening of abuse results in having time to reflect on the exact nature of the relationship. She is no longer so intensely involved with the business of self-preservation accompanied by defending and numbing herself. She now has time to think. Seeing the situation for what it is can serve to reinforce her commitment to leave. On the other hand, it is human nature to glorify the past by remembering the good more than the bad. If she does not have an immediate reminder of the extent of the abuse, reinforcement from the worker, often in graphic detail, is helpful. The continued case of Shirelle illustrates the need for reinforcement.

Shirelle came in for weekly appointments during her lunch hour. (Her husband would not question her because he knew sometimes she went out to lunch.) I told her she needed to speak to a lawyer since she thought her husband would contest the divorce. A friend had gotten divorced, and she wanted to use the friend's lawyer, although I suggested that she see a lawyer who specializes in domestic abuse cases. She was to see the lawyer between this appointment and our next.

During the week, Shirelle called to tell me she had "chickened out." I asked if she still wanted to leave her husband; she did. I encouraged her to see the lawyer. I asked if she could still make an appointment with a lawyer before she saw me next. She agreed that she would.

By the next appointment, she had seen the lawyer. This definite step, and a legal one at that, had frightened her, but she was glad she had taken it. The lawyer was a very tough and supportive woman who felt Shirelle was in a good position, relieving Shirelle immensely. She thought it would be hard paying the lawyer on her secretary's salary but was determined to find a way. I thought that was a good subject for us to talk about.

In addition to other areas she needed to develop a strategy for, one of them was finances, and we could start with the lawyer's fee. Although the lawyer would sue the husband and part of the divorce settlement would go toward the fee, the lawyer wanted a $1,000 retainer. Shirelle, biting her nails, asked, "Where am I going to get that?" We explored her options. She could take a loan from her credit union at work but was afraid that her husband might find out. She could not think of an alternative and looked defeated. Although I thought it was a long shot, I asked if she knew anyone she could borrow the money from—even small sums from different people. Shirelle did not think anyone she knew could spare money but suddenly said, "Wait a minute. My aunt works with me. She's in the credit union too. Maybe she could take it out, and I'll borrow it from her!" I told her that another option was to find a lawyer with a different financial arrangement. But she already liked this lawyer and wanted to stick with her.

Until she served her husband with divorce papers, she felt she could live with him and manage. But when the papers were served, she did not want to be around; she did not know what he would be capable of doing. We agreed that she should move as far away from him as possible. She would get an un-listed telephone and request that the telephone company not give her address to anyone. I suggested that once she had her apartment, she inform the local police precinct that her husband was violent and she had an order of protection. She should present the police with a copy of the order to keep on file.

By the next session, Shirelle had second thoughts. Her aunt had agreed to take the loan for her, but Shirelle became overwhelmed about all the money she would need; the $1,000 retainer was only the first step. She had realized that she would need a down payment of one month's rent as a security deposit plus the first month's rent, some furniture, and utility and telephone deposits. Since everything at home was in her husband's name, she had no credit; therefore, the various deposits were hefty. She put her head in her hands and blurted out, "Maybe I should just stay with him. Things are quiet now." Slowly and softly I said to her, "You can stay with him if you want. You have for a long time, and he has abused you for a long time. He's stopped before, but unfortunately, it's always started again." She sobbed, "I know. I don't want that anymore. I want to live in peace without worrying, but how am I going to do it?" I told her that there were ways she could get more money; she could begin to save and apply for her own credit card. That way she could charge things and even get a cash advance if need be. This relieved Shirelle somewhat. She said, "It will be slow, but I'll do it."

In the following session, Shirelle thought it would help her to get a second job but wondered how she could keep her husband from finding out. Although he would not object to her working two jobs—provided she still kept house and got his dinner on the table on time—he would want her to contribute more financially. I told her about a job corps for women that, among other things, trained women, free, in word processing. She already had typing skills and might qualify for it. She would then be able to freelance, working whatever hours she wanted and also be home if she so chose. Shirelle got excited about this possibility. She knew word processors made good money, and working whenever she wanted was ideal. Her husband worked the night shift; she could easily work in the evenings without his knowledge. She looked at me beaming: "Things are breaking right. I really feel this is the right thing to do."

Shirelle planned leaving in a step-by-step methodical way. Many times she had second thoughts. When she felt doubtful, she needed reinforcement from me that it would work out and that she was doing something in her own best interests. She made four attempts to leave but each time returned to her husband in response to his promises that things would be different. But Shirelle kept her savings account and credit card in her name, and she had her own financial resources when she finally left for good.

STAYING OUT

I received a call from a colleague who was referring a young couple, married one year, and there was violence in the relationship.

Dawn and David held management jobs in the corporate sector—in fact, that is how they met. They looked like the all-American couple but were not.

Dawn would start the violence. As David attempted to restrain her, he would get very angry and escalate the violence, which ended with his beating her. All attempts to stop the abuse failed. Dawn finally revealed to me in my sessions with both of them that David was an alcoholic, but he refused to acknowledge his addiction and refused to continue treatment with me or anyone else. I suggested that they separate; the violence was continuing, and David was denying. Dawn thought it was a good idea, but David did not. Dawn continued to see me but individually, and eventually she left David.

Although leaving David was an emotional hardship, Dawn was

able to pick up her life again. They had been married only a year, and she was financially independent. She wanted to continue counseling but preferred a different counselor. She lived far from my office and seeing me reminded her too much of her sessions with David. She thanked me for my help and terminated.

Three months later, she returned. Her sessions with her new counselor were not working well; moreover, David was continuing to ask her to come back to him, and she was weakening. She felt she needed to see me; I knew exactly how things were between them, and she felt that she needed me to remind her. The other counselor could talk to her about this but had no first-hand knowledge of their relationship, and I did.

Emotional, economic, and societal tugs to return to the partner are common. With the passing of time, the allure of the material comforts of home and the security attached to being coupled as opposed to being alone can seem appealing. Worse, the batterer may be urging the woman to come back. He may renew the courtship stage. He is on his best behavior, romancing her, expressing his need for her, and treating her well. Her old feelings for him may resurface, and she is often tempted to return.

In contrast to this romantic picture—what I call the idealized love stage—is a far different scenario but one that also may tempt her to return. Her partner may stalk, threaten, harass, or menace her. She may not be free to do anything—go to work or go out at night, for example—without his belligerent interference. He might call her day and night and even threaten to harm members of her family. In defeat, she grimly thinks of returning.

And there are several other possibilities as well. All, however, have as their common denominator the pull to return. The worker can be instrumental in strengthening the woman's determination to stay out by reminding her in graphic detail about the past. Early in counseling, I ask the woman to describe in detail, in writing or on a tape recorder, the worst incident of violence. When a woman is weakening, we reread the story to refreshen her memory of the violence. This is repeated as often as necessary, accompanied by supportive counseling, case management, and whatever other services she may need, using a multimodality treatment.

WHEN ONGOING TREATMENT IS ADVISED

Psychotherapy

After leaving her partner, a woman may feel insecure or frightened about repeating the past and picking another violent partner. She may want to examine the past violent relationship in detail and depth to learn from it in order to prevent a reoccurrence.

There is no consensus in the literature concerning why and how women get into battering relationships. Some researchers state that it is completely accidental. Others cite specific predispositions and/or family-of-origin causal factors. In all likelihood, there is no homogeneity: some battered women may accidentally find themselves in violent relationships, and for others, psychosocial and psychodynamic factors are contributory. Each woman must be viewed individually, with treatment plans tailored to her unique circumstances. When appropriate, treatment can focus in depth on underlying causality so that counterproductive past patterns, where they exist, are not repeated.

Posttraumatic Stress Disorder

A woman who has been battered may have a posttraumatic stress disorder reaction when she begins dating. The presence of a man or men in her life again may trigger past memories, with resulting traumatic responses; for example, if they argue, she may fear that it means he will become violent and she might become frozen with fear. He might be very attentive which she might misread as possessive and controlling, his desire to see her might be misconstrued as intrusive, and so on. In such cases, short-term treatment, focused on the trauma and working through her reactions, is beneficial.

Couples Therapy

Once a woman is involved in another relationship, couples therapy may prove useful. It may help her adjust to a new relationship and can be helpful to her new partner for him to know about her past trauma. His presence in sessions can help him to understand and be responsive to her. The case of Anne demonstrates the effectiveness of in-depth treatment following the aftermath of ending a violent relationship.

Anne had successfully ended an abusive relationship and made a new life for herself. She continued to see me for psychotherapy sessions once a week, at her request. Anne, at 35, recognized that she had a history of relationships that were abusive, although never before had they been physically violent. All of her past relationships had been characterized by a lot of conflict, dramatic breakups, passionate reconciliations, and ultimate severing of ties. She felt there was a counterproductive pattern that she wanted to avoid in the future. Both her age and the violence in her previous relationship jarred her into the realization that she needed to make changes.

During the course of treatment, Anne recognized that she was repeating childhood experiences. Her father, an alcoholic, had always argued with her mother. Although there was no physical violence between them, the arguments, when he was drinking, became verbally abusive. The five children learned to stay out of the way. Anne also had had a negative relationship with her mother, who berated and belittled her and often blamed her for intrafamily problems. One example she told to me was about her brother, two years younger. He was a model child, well behaved and cooperative, as contrasted to the "brat" she was, as her mother often told her. But he finally rebelled, becoming hostile and belligerent. Anne was told that her bad character had rubbed off on him. In response, she tuned out household conflicts and, in fact, until the treatment, had blocked out these events. When she reached adolescence, she rebelled, becoming defiant and disobedient. Her mother tried to set limits, but Anne nevertheless did as she pleased. They argued a lot, and now Anne followed her mother's example, berating and belittling her mother.

In retrospect, Anne felt bad about how she had treated her mother but at the time had hardened herself to her feelings, acting as if she did not care. She finally realized that her relationships with men resembled her relationship with her mother. At the age of 35, she was able to allow herself to feel and found her behavior with men to be emotionally uncomfortable. She began visiting her parents and was able to observe their interactions with an objectivity she had lacked while growing up and also to note her interactions with her mother.

She started to date again but was wary of getting involved for fear her past would repeat itself. We analyzed the men she was with, as well as her behavior and feelings. Most of the relationships were short-lived as she tested herself. She became aware of her feelings and how she created distance in relationships because she was afraid. She followed a pattern of dating, followed by periods of abstinence when she analyzed what had happened and what she wanted to change. She got closer and closer to finding a more suitable partner. Eventually she met a man she could trust and began a long-term relationship with him.

Although they did not go into couples' treatment, he was understanding, perceptive, and patient. She was open with him, sharing her fears and doubts. Both were committed to resolving the problems in the relationship. He had better communication skills than she, but she was able to take information from her individual sessions and share it with him.

We have not reached the end of the story, since this case is current. Whatever the outcome for Anne, she understands the connection between her past and her present. She has developed adequate self-awareness to deal with repetition compulsion. She is now motivated to be in a healthy relationship. Not all women who terminate battering relationships may need or want psychotherapy, but for those who do, the outcome can be beneficial.

The techniques I have described in this chapter combine the use of several approaches applied simultaneously or separately as needed. The multimodality approach enables the worker to change techniques as the case progresses, offering the client concrete as well as psychotheraputic approaches and can be applied individually or in groups. For women who get out of battering relationships, another approach is a self-help support group which can help sustain her staying out. The type of women's group described in the next chapter for women still in the relationship can prove helpful to both women who have left abusive relationships and those who have stayed. Women who have left can learn from the others and be an inspiration for women who have stayed; women who have stayed serve as a sharp reminder of these relationships for the women who have left. In the next chapter I will explore groups for women who remain in the abusive relationship.

4

Staying

Support and Survival Skills Training Groups

A woman named Cynthia called saying that she and her boyfriend had a lot of fights. It had gotten to the point where she could not stand it anymore. She heard that we could help her.

I asked Cynthia what happened when they fight, and she replied, "He gets loud and stuff like that." "Stuff like that" meant he became violent. I thought it was good that she did not want to stand for it anymore and told her that she had come to the right place; we could help her. First, I needed a little more information from her.

Cynthia and her boyfriend had been living together for seven years and had two children and he had been abusive the length of time they had been together. The police had been called several times, always by the neighbors. When they arrived, either Dirk, Cynthia's boyfriend, had already fled, or the police would tell him to cool down and take a walk. Lately, he came home drunk and then kept her up all night, yelling at and accusing her. The pattern of violence had intensified, prompting this call.

I told Cynthia she had several options: she could leave him, and we would help her with this (I told her about shelters); she could have him come in, and we would work on stopping the abuse; she could stay with him and get an order of protection

37

that might deter his violence; or she could come in for counseling and try to figure out what she wanted. She was not prepared to make a specific decision, although she did not want to leave him. She had tried that before and always returned; in spite of the abuse, she thought life was better with him than without him. She knew about shelters and orders of protection. She had the latter once, and it did not do any good, so she let it expire. She would like him to come in but did not think he would. Cynthia said that in his culture, it was not wrong "to slap a woman around." His father had beaten his mother, and his brothers beat their women. She wanted a chance to talk to someone and figure out what to do.

I told Cynthia that she could see a counselor or come to our women's group; the latter seemed to interest her, and she asked about the group. I told her that we met two hours a week, and there were seven women in the group with problems similar to hers. The women talked about their concerns and learned more about domestic violence, including how to protect themselves. She said she did not want to be "condemned" for not leaving Dirk. I assured her that would not happen; many of the women in the group were still living with their partners.

Cynthia was an excellent candidate for a women's support and survival skills training group. She was entrenched in an abusive relationship, she had strong ties to this man, she had unsuccessfully tried to leave him, she had children with him, and, most important at the moment of the call, she had no desire to leave him. She had prior experience with orders of protection and the police and felt those avenues were not useful to her. Her boyfriend was an unlikely candidate for help: he was drinking heavily, did not see anything wrong with his behavior, and violence was accepted in his subculture. She was uncertain about what she wanted to do about the situation, which probably indicated that she was not ready to take a specific action. The group would give her an opportunity to think and to learn, to meet with other women in her situation, to expand her options, and, of great importance, to learn how to protect herself better against the violence through survival skills training. In other words, the group would be empowering.

THE GROUP EXPERIENCE

Groups have proved beneficial psychologically and economically. I. Yalom has developed eleven postulates on the advantages of group treatment that provide a therapeutic experience. Here I summarize them into their most rudimentary form:

1. *Instillation of hope,* which relates to the client's belief that being a member of the group will be helpful. Calling attention to improvements that members have made provides hope to the others that they can improve too.

2. *Universality.* When members hear that others in the group are having the same experiences, they do not feel as socially isolated. It is tremendously relieving to members to know they are not alone.

3. *Imparting of information,* where explanation and clarification are therapeutic, for says Yalom, "the explanation of a phenomenon is the first step toward its control."

4. *Altruism.* People beginning therapy think they have nothing to offer anyone else; they have become demoralized by the burdens of their own problems. In a group, the realization that they are important to others boosts their self-esteem.

5. *The corrective recapitulation of the primary family group.* The group becomes a family of sorts. Members can have a more positive experience with group members as family than they had in their own families.

6. *Development of socializing techniques,* important for people lacking intimate relationships.

7. *Imitative behavior.* Group members can learn how to behave by imitating other members' behavior.

8. *Interpersonal learning.* People who come to group therapy have experienced disturbances in their interpersonal relationships and can learn more productive ways of relating through the group experience, which "evolves into a social microcosm, a miniaturized representation of each patient's social universe."

9. *Group cohesiveness,* a major source of help to members because of the acceptance received from other members of the group. The positive outcome of the group is directly related to the level of cohesiveness of the group.

10. *Catharsis.* Strong expressions of emotion by group members coupled with group cohesiveness result in close mutual bonds among group members. The value of catharsis is in the strong bonds that form between the members and lead to greater closeness between them.

11. *Existential factors.* Members learn that there are limits to others' ability to help them. Each person is ultimately responsible for his or her own life. There is a basic aloneness to existence that cannot be avoided.[1]

These eleven factors provide the framework in which group therapy takes place. Yalom's theory thus lays the foundation for group treatment for battered women.*

THE VALUE OF A GROUP FOR BATTERED WOMEN

Battered women do not easily or readily reveal the abuse because they feel to blame and ashamed. They may have internalized attitudes about themselves that blame and shun them for the abuse. Additionally, they may be caught in the psychological web of the battered woman syndrome, the Stockholm syndrome, and posttraumatic stress disorder. As a result of these feelings of self-blame and shame, they withdraw from others, hiding their problems and being secretive about the abuse. Their partners may isolate them further by restricting where they can go and with whom and by limiting finances, the use of the car, how much they can talk on the telephone and to whom, and so forth. If they suffer from visible bruises, they might not go out of the house, increasing their isolation.

When battered women join a group, the first benefit is the opportunity to break the pattern of isolation. Second, the group can strengthen self-esteem. Battered women often suffer from low self-esteem, which typically results from the physical and psychological abuse. Psychological abuse entails their partners belittling them, demeaning them, blaming them, confusing them, and threatening them. Women report that the psychological abuse is often worse than

---

*All but one of the factors that Yalom delineates can find application to groups for battered women. Factor 8, interpersonal learning, is not relevant in my opinion. There is no evidence to show that, with the exception of their relationship with their partner, there is a disturbance in interpersonal relationships. The factors affecting a poor relationship with a woman's partner relate to his being a batterer rather than necessarily a flaw in her ability to relate interpersonally.

the physical.[2] Over time, their self-esteem can be eroded. One of the stages of victimization, according to Symonds, is psychological infantilism; the victim clings to her abuser and feels grateful to and needy of him. During this stage, her self-esteem plummets.[3] The supportive aspect of the group and group cohesiveness enhances self-esteem. A woman can look around and see that other battered women have positive and admirable traits, which she can identify with as well as receive validation from others that she is not the dishrag, slob, or slut her partner has been calling her.

Third, the peer group support and networking available are empowering. Group members often continue much-needed contact with one another outside the group, both between sessions and after termination. By hearing other women's experiences and sometimes their solutions, women are given an opportunity to broaden their vision and consider a range of options. As a result of the group experience, sometimes women who felt resigned and reconciled to the domestic violence can make changes. Some women take control to stop the abuse by leaving their partners, obtaining orders of protection, or getting their partners to come for help.

Fourth, the group provides the opportunity to educate women about the reasons for violence. Most battered women internalize society's attitudes about why they are battered, as well as the reasons their partners give for battering them; both blame the victim. In the group, women hear about the acceptance of violence on a societal level, and they realize that the responsibility for violence is placed on the men, thus helping to free the women from self-recrimination. Finally, one of the most critical aspects of the group is the learning of survival skills training to help women protect themselves against abuse.

THE GROUP EXPERIENCE

What the Group Cannot Do

The group experience cannot prevent violence, and often it cannot prevent women from living with violence. Violence ceases only when the batterer gets help or when women take measures to end violence in their lives, usually by leaving or taking legal action.

The grim reality is that the majority of women who come to women's groups will remain in the relationship, and violence will reoccur. Readers must be cautioned about high expectations and the frustration and discouragement that result when expectations do not reach fruition. Although goals must be modified, they are nonetheless meaningful.

Ruling Out Women from the Group

Assessment and differential diagnosis need to be made to determine a client's suitability for a battered women's group. Not every battered woman benefits from the same approach. Sometimes practitioners seem to equate "battered" with women's group placement. Certainly many abused women will benefit from the group experience, but not all will. Care must be taken to determine suitability of group placement. People who are inappropriately assigned to a group are unlikely to benefit from the experience and may also adversely affect the group.[4]

Certain psychiatric diagnoses like acute psychosis and some forms of paranoia could rule out group treatment,* as would instances in which a group would be threatening—typically when there is denial, when subcultural values conflict with group values, or when the person's personality makeup is not condusive to group treatment.

Denial

Some women may know that they are abused but be unable to admit to it fully. They might go for help on an individual basis, but being with other women in a group whose major purpose is to discuss abuse may be too threatening. They have erected self-defenses against the idea that they are battered and may not be able to tolerate the association with women who openly admit to partner abuse. Yalom's term for this is the "fear of emotional contagion." Some people are "extremely adversely affected by hearing the problems of the other group members" because they see themselves in others.[5]

*For guidelines, please see the *Diagnostic & Statistical Manual of Mental Disorders*. Washington, D.C. American Psychiatric Press, 1980.

The result could be that they would fortify their defenses still further or even drop out of treatment.

Subcultural Values

In certain cultures, women feel that sharing personal information about family matters, especially about their relationship with their husbands, is shameful and disrespectful. The expectation of talking to a group of strangers about their partner would repel these women, who would more than likely drop out of treatment.

Personality

Groups are not for everyone. Some people are not comfortable with sharing personal problems in a group; they are likely to remain silent and feel uncomfortable.

Suitable Candidates for Womens' Groups

Suitable members for a women's group are women who want to try this mode of treatment. Other suitable candidates are women who do not want to or cannot be seen with their partners, either because it is too dangerous, they are planning to leave, their partners cannot benefit from treatment, or their partners do not want help. If women are not ruled out of group, then they are suitable. Women whose partners are receiving help may be in group as well.

GROUP CONSIDERATIONS

Monday 9:00 A.M.: a call from a woman named Chris. Sobbing, she said that her husband had just beaten her. I discussed whether she was safe and her need for medical care. Since he had already left for work, she was safe for the time being. She said that she did not need or want a doctor but wanted help right away. I thought about the women's group I was trying to

form but I did not have enough potential members yet. I invited
her to come in.

Starting the Group

The first dilemma faced by workers in starting a women's group is
starting: how do you get enough women together at the same time?
An ideal-sized group is eight to ten members, taking absences into
account. Five members can be comfortable and intimate as well;
therefore, the group can begin when there are five women.

In traditional therapy or counseling, the practitioner probably has
the luxury of placing potential group members on a waiting list until
there are enough people to begin. But battering has a time-critical
aspect to it requiring immediate intervention, as Chris's case
showed. Placing women on a waiting list often proves counterproductive.

Until the group is ready to begin, the counselor can offer three
options: in-person individual counseling, telephone contact, or a
waiting-list group. For all three, women need to be told that this is a
temporary measure until the full group is ready. The worker should
make frequent reference to the group so that the women are assured
that it will really happen.

Interim Interventions

Individual Counseling in person or by telephone

Until the group's start-up, each woman can be seen individually by
the group leader. The leader and the woman need a chance to get to
know one another, which helps to establish rapport and assess
suitability for the group. The client has an opportunity to ask
questions about the group, be inducted into the group culture, and
examine whether she thinks the group is a good choice. The leader
can gather information about the woman that helps to assess her
suitability for this treatment. The worker explains how the group
operates and its rules and regulations (the group culture). These
individual sessions can be a relief for the woman; they acquaint her
with the leader (she does not know anyone else in the group) and let

her know what to expect. The leader can create a bridge from her life outside the group to her life inside it.

When Chris came in, her immediate needs were attended to. A determination of physical safety was obtained, which included whether her home was safe for her and whether she needed medical attention. The pattern of abuse with her husband meant that after a battering episode, he was not violent for several weeks; therefore, she felt there was no immediate danger, and she could return home. I checked her injuries by asking what he had done to her. Chris did not seem to need or want medical care, but she did want to talk. She was upset over the violence and needed an opportunity to tell her story to someone with a listening and supportive ear. She was simultaneously outraged and hurt, expressing anger and crying. I obtained a history of the abuse as well as information about the relationship. It was only at this point that Chris was ready to hear the range of options available. She did not want to give up on the relationship but did not think that her husband would come for help. I explained that his violence could not be stopped just by Chris's being seen. Either he had to get help, or she could try obtaining an order of protection, which in some cases deters violence (I explained the limits of an order of protection too). Chris wanted to see if an order of protection would work, and I helped her plan how to obtain one. Finally, I told her about the women's group that was forming and invited her to join, offering her continued contact in person or on the telephone, as needed.

Individual counseling in person or on the telephone as an interim intervention until a women's group begins entails supportive techniques, information and referral, and the teaching of survival skills. Formation of group might take several weeks while waiting to build membership, and the women who are waiting should not be left hanging. The worker provides the essential services until the group begins, mentioning the group frequently so that the women know the group is expected to start shortly. Talking about the group may also prevent the women from losing interest due to the delay. Supportive services include believing her, being sympathetic to her situation, conveying willingness to advocate for her needs, being emotionally available to her, encouraging attempts toward empowerment, listening, and acceptance.

Information and referral requires knowledge of community resources and resources for battered women. It might entail legal, medical, vocational, housing (permanent and temporary), financial, child care, and use of the human services network.

Waiting List Group

The women waiting for the regular group to begin can be seen periodically in what I call a "waiting list group," until circumstances permit the actual group to begin. Infrequent meetings are more efficient than meeting individually with the women on the waiting list; they provide for continuity; they help bring about group cohesiveness; and they help maintain the connection between the women and the worker. Moreover, the frequency with which clients are seen before entering the group affects the rate of dropouts from the group.[6]

Battered women cannot be put on a waiting list, with no service given. Most do not easily and readily call for service. When they do, they must be helped, or they are likely to be lost, either temporarily until the next battering episode or permanently because they have been killed. Further, if they are calling in crisis, they cannot wait. It is unconscionable to respond to what may be a woman's only cry for help with the answer, "You will be placed on the waiting list." Offering interim interventions until service can begin is a reasonable and necessary compromise.

Techniques of Crisis Intervention

When women in crisis call for help, it is appropriate for the worker to apply techniques of crisis intervention. Crisis involves a breakdown in coping mechanisms.[7] The purpose of crisis intervention is to solve the immediate and presenting problem. It is to be used upon the threat of or actual violence.

The first step is to help the woman to calm down. A few deep breaths, comforting statements from the worker, or other relaxation techniques may help. Once she is calmer, the next step is to determine the need for physical safety, which includes whether her environment is safe and whether she is in need of medical attention. Is she standing on a street corner? Does she have somewhere safe to go? Can she return to her home? Careful questioning in detail is important. During a crisis, people's thought processes often lack clarity; the woman's judgment might be impaired temporarily, and she may minimize or deny the extent of danger. In a crisis, the counselor needs to exercise judgment about the woman's environmental and personal safety as well.

When I met Maria, she was sobbing and shivering and huddled close to her friend who had a comforting arm around her. She had black circles around her eyes where her eye makeup had smeared from her tears. Caked blood on her upper arm was visible through her torn sleeve. I invited Maria and her friend into the office.

I waited a few minutes before beginning because Maria was crying so hard. I gently asked if either would like a cup of tea, broth, or coffee and brought them what they wanted. After a few sips, Maria looked up at me; her sobs had stopped, although tears continued to stream down her cheeks. I asked if she would like to wash up a little, to which she nodded her head. After she and her friend returned from the bathroom, I said that I would like to see her upper arm. It turned out that it was just a scratch but looked more serious with the caked blood. She had been hurt by a rough edge on a metal bookcase when her husband pushed her and pinned her against the bookcase. After her husband punched and slapped her for several minutes, she finally managed to get out of his grasp and run out of the house. She ran the three blocks to her friend, who suggested that they come here.

I was concerned about her arm and the question of tetanus and asked if she would like medical attention, to which she said no. She minimized the situation and preferred to talk.

She said she could not take this anymore, telling me he had done things like this for many years. I asked how many years, obtaining a history of the abuse. Her friend told her it was "enough already" and she should leave him, a comment that led to a heated discussion between the two of them. I interrupted to say I could tell her about her options and what she could do. She did not want to follow through on anything, saying his mother would talk to him and he would stop. I explained how violence between partners usually escalates and increases in frequency and intensity over time. Battering is like a disease, I told her, which left untreated, would probably get worse. I expressed concern for her future safety. I also doubted that his mother's talking to him would result in his stopping. My remarks were punctuated with her friend's saying, "You see," "I told you," "Right," "Listen to her Maria," and the like. When I finished, she said she wanted to think it over, and she would come back again tomorrow; right now, she wanted to go home.

I asked if she would be safe at home. (She was not thinking about her safety but just her desire to rest.) She was not sure, so I told her about shelters providing a safe haven and supportive services. But she still wanted to go to her own home today, saying he would probably stay away from home for a few days. We talked about precautions she could take. I suggested that she think over the options and we would talk again tomorrow. I urged her to get her arm looked at because I was concerned about it. She thought she might after a few hours of sleep. I suggested she do it now, after leaving here, on her way home. I thought she would sleep more peacefully if she took care of herself medically, and while she was there, she should have a medical examination. She had insurance and seemed agreeable. I suggested a private doctor whom I knew understood about domestic violence, and, with her consent, I called him, telling him to expect Maria. Her friend said, "I'll go with you Maria."

Although I had mentioned the women's group, I did not suggest joining it because Maria had no desire to think about services at that time. Since she planned to meet with me the next day and since she was still in trauma, deciding about options could be postponed (although options were explored). The priority for personal safety in her case was attended to in her agreement to get medical attention. Although Maria thought she would be safe at home, I outlined precautions to take—how to get police protection and a plan for escape should her husband become violent again—in the event being at home proved threatening.

Group Composition

Another issue for start-up is whether the group should be homogeneous. How similar in age, life-style, ethnicity, cultural background, and other demographics should members be?

Unless one is dealing with a very tightly knit and closed population with rigid customs and prohibitions that separate them from the larger society (such as Orthodox Jews, the Amish, or Jehovah Witnesses), the common denominator of battering unifies the women. Moreover, there is value in heterogeneity. Members who are different from each other bring their differences to the group, enriching the group as a whole. It is not uncommon for an older woman to befriend and even nurture a younger member or for someone whose subculture sanctions battering to learn it is not a universal sanction. Women who have left an abusive relationship can be mixed with those who are still in such a relationship, with each profiting. Women who have left the home need continued support to stay out. Women still in the battering relationship serve as reminders to women of the reality of the relationship. For women still living with abuse, interacting with women who have left demonstrates that leaving is possible, and they can learn from those who have left.

Closed versus Open Groups

A closed group means that once a certain number of women join, no new members are allowed in or are allowed only with careful consideration. The members make a commitment to the group. Group cohesiveness and identity are very strong, with members heavily invested in maintaining the group's life. Group process, meaning here how the group unfolds and develops over time based on the members' interaction, becomes a major tool.

In an open group, members come and go, with new women accepted at any time. Usually there is a core membership who attend regularly and induct new members into the group. The cohesiveness develops as a result of sharing a common problem. Group identity and investment in the life of the group is lessened, there is less commitment, and the ability to use group process is diminished.

There are advantages and disadvantages to both types of group. A closed group maximizes Yalom's eleven primary factors. The group progresses from week to week, and therapeutic work is in depth. One disadvantage is that it limits the number of women to be helped. Another disadvantage is that new members, once admitted to the group, may feel uncomfortable being new. Taking in new women regularly, as is done in an open group, has the advantage of being able to serve any woman who needs help and a disadvantage, the feeling for both the members and the leader is that the group is always starting at the beginning; each time a new woman enters, she has to be incorporated into the group through the introductory process. Both closed and open groups have proved effective. The choice is up to the practitioner.

The Meeting Schedule

I recommend that the group have a fixed schedule, with the time and day the group meets made clear to the women. If women are making arrangements that may be difficult for them, they are owed the consideration of consistency. Beyond that, they need the constancy in what are otherwise chaotic lives. If they are to make a commitment to the group, so must the leader. Cancelling or changing the group time and day is not conducive to commitments. Finally, it is comforting to women to know on which day and at what time they can talk about and get help for the violence in their lives.

The specific schedule can be worked out with either the members or decided by the leader. The group model that I am presenting calls for a weekly meeting lasting two hours. How frequently the group meets can be decided based on the idiosyncratic nature of a particular circumstance but not the amount of time. The goals to be accomplished cannot occur in less than two hours. More than two hours is hard on the leader and may be unmanageable for the women because of time away from their primary responsibilities.

GROUP FORMAT

The leader plays an active role in determining how the group will proceed. Group format has two aspects: the structural design and what the members do.

Structural Considerations

Physically, a pleasant room, with no intrusions (telephones ringing, other people's conversations, or interruptions) and with privacy is preferable. The women need to feel that the time is only for them. Privacy is often rare in their lives; certainly, their partners do not allow them their own space. They are used to being intruded upon.

The group time needs to be different. I have found that respecting and creating privacy is healing in and of itself. For the same reasons, I recommend that the leader be present to the entire group and not be distracted by other demands. The women need to know that they are important and their issues are being seriously considered.

Chairs in a circle, with no chair behind another, is the optimal placement. People can see one another in a circle, and symbolically a circle forms a whole. The leader's chair should be the same height as everyone else's so she is neither above nor below the group members but on an equal plane. Battered women are particularly aware of power issues; their partners use physical force to overpower them. A power differential does exist between the leader and the women by the fact that the leader is a paid professional and not one of them, but the difference should be minimized where appropriate.[8]

Refreshments may or may not be served. If they are available, they should be simple so as not to distract from the purpose of the group.

The desired atmosphere is one where the women feel physically and emotionally comfortable. The group may be their only safe haven. Wearing casual clothes or kicking off shoes may be signs that the women feel at ease.

Confidentiality

Workers are familiar with issues of confidentiality. Group members, however, may not be as concerned regarding sharing information about other members outside the group. In the case of battered women, repeating information about a member outside the group could be dangerous. Can a member be sure that information she is passing on about another woman will not get back to that woman's partner, her friends, or her children? For safety, no member should repeat information shared inside the group outside it.

The Silent Member

Different philosophies prevail concerning reaching out to a silent member of a group for the purpose of engaging her. Initially, it is ill advised to encourage a silent woman to share. A battered woman pushed to speak might experience this as abusive. Her partner forces her to behave in a certain way. She might view the group leader's probing not as helping her to enter the group but as force and coercion. My recommendation is to wait until the third session before attempting to engage a reticent member. If she still resists attempts at engagement, her hesitation should be respected. The leader can approach her outside the group on a one-to-one basis in an attempt to engage her. It is common for other group members to reach out to her. She may also be drawn into the group by outreach efforts of peers.

GROUP OBJECTIVES

Objective 1: Combating Isolation

When a battered woman joins a woman's group, this may be the first time that she has freely been able to share her troubles with her peers. Many battered women, ashamed of the abuse, do not tell their friends. And even if they do, friends who are not abused may not empathize with her. They may not be able to offer the support she needs because they cannot understand what it feels like to be hit by the person one loves; they may even be unsympathetic or hostile.

In a group, the woman is with others who know from first-hand experience what she is going through—a relief and a comfort. A woman sometimes thinks she is the only one being abused. Feeling alone often adds to her feelings of shame and self-recrimination, further isolating her. Knowing that other women are abused can lessen her sense of aloneness, which makes her feel estranged and different from others.

After a battering episode, many women do not leave the house because of their bruises. They avoid contact with others in order not to be questioned about their injuries. Sometimes they are so traumatized by the violence that they cannot communicate with others. Women whose partners isolate them are forbidden to interact. The act of entering the group changes the pattern of isolation before any other intervention is attempted.

Objective 2: Strengthening Self-Esteem

Battering assaults self-esteem. Early studies of battered women concluded that they had poor self-esteem. Subsequent study revealed that the effects of the violence caused a change in self-esteem. A batterer puts up a number of defenses:

1. He externalizes the problem by blaming his partner for the abuse and claims it is her fault, conveying that she cannot do things right. Eventually she believes him, and her self-esteem drops.

2. He denies that he is at fault, often seeing himself instead of her as the victim. She joins in his denial, wanting to believe that there are good reasons for the abuse and he is not to blame. She has a desire to believe that the abuse is temporary and that she can influence the outcome. She has been socialized into believing that a woman's role is to make the marriage work.[9] Her beliefs lead her to try to stop the abuse, but to no avail. She views this failed attempt as her failure—another blow to her self-esteem.

3. In most cases, after a batterer has abused his partner and when the period of remorse is over, he minimizes the harm to her. But she knows how traumatic it was and can only feel diminished by his playing down of violence, affecting her self-esteem.

4. He rationalizes his responsibility for the abuse by blaming her for needing to be violent. His constant blaming of her affects her self-esteem. He tells her how bad a person she is, conveying a negative image of her.

5. He projects his own thoughts and feelings. Based on the lack of appropriate response from society, she internalizes his view of her, affecting her self-esteem. As the battering increases in frequency and intensity, her ability to cope drops; her functioning is affected, often resulting in decreased accomplishments, which affects her self-esteem.

The group offers an opportunity for positive feedback and a challenge to her belief in the batterer's defenses. The members directly challenge the beliefs she has come to accept. They support and strengthen her feelings about herself. Moreover, through association with the women in the group, she will experience and then identify with their strengths. Recognizing that other battered women have positive attributes will reflect on her feelings about herself and improve her self-esteem.

One woman told me that her husband called her stupid, giving her elaborate reasons. He told her that no one else would want her; he was the only one who would put up with her stupidity. Her mother used to say similar things to her. When she had dropped out of high school, against her mother's wishes, her mother said the only option for her was to get married and let her husband make the decisions for her. She interpreted this to mean she was too dumb to think for herself.

In the group, she learned that other women whom she considered smart were called "stupid" by their partners. She also helped work out a plan for one of the women that required complicated strategies. She initiated the suggestion and developed the plan. The feedback she got from the group conveyed how smart they thought she was. Although her husband continued to repeat the litany about her stupidity, she saw the insults as his attempts to demean her and disenfranchise her. They no longer had a negative affect on her feelings about her intelligence. The group supported her new view of herself, counterbalancing her husband's view. Her experiences in the group had a positive effect on her self-esteem.

Objective 3: Peer Group Support and Networking

Women's groups are supportive in nature. They enhance members' self-esteem, and the members provide support to one another. Women experience sharing a common problem as supportive, and often strong bonds develop in the group.

Battered women are not given adequate support in society at large, so the group may be the only place where these women feel understood. Moreover, the women are accepted and valued for who they are, in direct contrast to how their partners and the systems view them.

In the group, women are not blamed for being battered, for staying in the relationship, or for not taking steps to change the situation. Every woman has been given acceptance to be in whatever place she is. Acceptance is passed on to other members and becomes a group value. Not being blamed is a relief to these women. It releases them from guilt, self-recrimination, and maybe even self-hatred. Blame is immobilizing and counterproductive; it becomes internalized, often resulting in depression and apathy, and it prevents change. A woman who is relieved of blame and understands the ramifications of the problem of battering is freed to broaden her vision. She is given opportunity in the group to hear about and from other battered women, to discover their solutions, and to examine how their experience applies to her.

Objective 4: Expanding the Range of Options and Providing Information and Referral

Information and referral concerning community services available to battered women becomes a group topic. It is important for the leader to be knowledgeable about the resources, to have experience about what works, to understand how to get the systems to work effectively, to know which people in the system will provide smooth entry, and to understand the realistic limits to the systems.

I have found that policies and procedures on paper are often very different in reality. For example, on paper, a woman who is battered can call the police for protection. In reality, the police are often unresponsive, and any response may be inadequate. A group leader, unmindful of this discrepancy will provide misleading and perhaps injurious information. Following the paper procedure will not work, and the woman may interpret this lack of effectiveness as proof that the domestic violence cannot be stopped. The feedback the woman has gotten is that the systems do not work. She is powerless to stop him, and so are the systems she has used to try to stop him. This failure dashes a hope that has been fanned by being told in the group that there are ways to stop the battering and renews feelings of helplessness.

Leaders can learn strategies that will result in an effective response to the systems so that what is on paper will be carried out in practice. (Chapter 7 describes strategies that I have found to be effective in New York City. Workers need to learn what strategies will work in their area.) Or they can make an appropriate referral to someone in the community who can do this. Working with battered women means involvement on a community level, as well as involvement in treatment. Although group members provide information about effective use of the systems based on their experience, leaders themselves should know where to turn.

Many battered women are unaware of the resources available to them and how to use them. Information about resources shared in the group broadens their view concerning what they can do about their situation, expands the range of their options, may lessen feelings of being locked in and trapped, and may result in a referral to the resources.

Another means of expanding the range of options is through sharing of information about other available counseling modalities, such as transitional counseling for women planning to leave or who have left, interventions with batterers either individually or in groups, and couples work. As a result of participation in the women's group, some women decide to leave their situation or encourage their partners to get help. As battered women's needs change, the methods of help change too. With the multimodality approach, women can choose from a range of options.

Objective 5: Educating Women About Male Violence

Battered women need educating about the nature of violence and who is responsible for its perpetuation. The group is an excellent vehicle for this educating about male violence.

Discussion can begin with the broader issue of the acceptance of violence on a societal level, which includes tolerating it in child-rearing practices.[10] It is societally acceptable for parents to discipline children by hitting them. Children are being disciplined in this manner by people who love and take care of them and whom they love in turn. Parents also have more power and control than children. Pain, power, and love can thus become confused in a child's mind. Pain as a by-product of love can be viewed as sanctioned. It is possible that for some adults, the acceptance of violence may be connected to the experiences with discipline learned as a child. To counteract this attitude, the group leader can present feminist thinking concerning the relationship of men and women, where women are viewed as second-class and not equal and the power brokers are men. The discussion can focus on the clinical view that some men do not know how to deal with aggressive feelings in nonviolent ways and need to be taught alternatives. Batter-er responsibility must be emphasized, and the notion that the batterer has a choice about how he expresses anger needs to be explored.

The leader's focus on an analysis of violence and societal toleration of it, as well as reasons men batter, can help deflect blame away from the women. The leader emphasizes that the battering is the sole responsibility of the batterer, and how he responds to anger is his choosing. Emphasizing batterer responsibility for violence can help women not to excuse the violence and take blame for it because he was "provoked." Education about male violence may help her to realize that she is not responsible for his violence. The fault lies elsewhere.

Objective 6: Teaching Survival Skills Strategies

Women who remain in a violent relationship need help in coping with the battering. The worker's goal here is limited—but vital. The choice of staying or leaving a battering relationship is the woman's. No one can force the woman to make a decision that she neither wants to make nor is ready to make. Every woman in the group needs to know that her choice to stay or leave is respected. To try to force decisions is, at best, denying her the right to determine her own fate and, at worst, coercive. The leader should explain that women sometimes practice leaving for a long time before they actually make the break permanently, and many women never leave; both are accepted.[11] Even though they remain with the batterer, they can be helped to cope with the situation better.

Workers need to resensitize women because they often numb themselves to the batterings and develop a plan of escape with them. This is done in the women's group.

Sensitization Techniques

Most batterers give signals indicating their anger is escalating to violence; perhaps their face reddens and their fists clench. The woman must learn to note those signs.

Within the group, the leader has an individual strategy sheet (see Exhibit 4–1) for every woman on which her survival plan will be delineated. The leader then asks each woman if her partner gives any physical signs and notes them in detail, while writing down what each woman has said on that woman's strategy sheet. Then the women are

---

DATE _____   NAME _____

1. BATTERER'S SIGNALS   2. HOW CAN ANGER BE AVOIDED?

3. WHERE CAN YOU GO   4. WHAT FINANCIAL RESOURCES
   TO BE SAFE?   ARE AVAILABLE FOR ESCAPE?

5. WHERE WILL YOU KEEP   6. WHAT IS YOUR PLAN FOR
   MONEY, ETC?   YOUR CHILDREN?

7. ADDITIONAL COMMENTS:

8. STEP-BY-STEP SURVIVAL/ESCAPE PLAN
   a.
   b.
   c.
   d.
   e.

Exhibit 4–1   *Survival Skills Strategy Sheet for Women's Groups*

asked what they can do to avoid the anger once it begins. Any strategy the woman notes is written down. For example, women are encouraged to let others come to their aid and plan to intervene in order to disrupt the escalation. An innocent knock on the door by a receptive neighbor may be enough to interrupt the violence, or a child may have to get some help. (Children should not intervene directly. They cannot do so effectively with an adult and can get hurt in the process, accidentally or on purpose. Nevertheless, they may be able to play a role in getting some outside help.) A specific plan for notifying the neighbor or what signal to use with the neighbor so that he or she knows when to intervene needs to be developed. Women may not readily want to turn to someone else for aid because of their shame about being battered. As they become less ashamed and stop blaming themselves, they may be more willing to ask for assistance.

Some women may be able to diffuse the anger or be taught how to do so—perhaps by leaving the room, stopping the discussion, or appeasing the batterer. Each woman needs to examine what will work in her case.

Escape Plan

Many women report that there is no way to stop the anger once it begins; these women need an escape plan. (We do not consider here women who are trapped by the batterer and have no exit. For women whose partners pull out the telephone, block their exits, and pin them down, there is probably no escape from the violent episode. The only relief comes after the violence ends.)

Women who can break free and leave need to leave for somewhere. Is there a place they can go where they will be safe: a shelter, a friend, or a hotel? Women can plan to keep with them at all times a credit card, a subway token, money pinned to their underwear, the car keys, and so forth.

The escape plan is individualized for each woman based on her circumstances and written down on her strategy sheet. Children need to be prepared to leave. They can be drilled in what they are to do if they are old enough, or a plan must be made for someone to take care of them. All of this is written down.

Women may want to rely on their own resources first, such as access to money to stay at a hotel or family or friends who can safely take them in. The use of one's own resources allows for the most comfort and predictability.

Some women may prefer or need to use community resources such as shelters. The limitations to shelters, however, are that there may not be room, rules may seem too restrictive, or the shelter may be in a community far from a woman's home. On the other hand, shelters are designed with battered women's needs in mind. The staff is expert at dealing with the problem, the facility is safe, and the presence of other battered women offers the benefits described in the battered women's group. The group leader needs to be prepared with information about shelters.

After each strategy plan is developed and written down, the

worker reviews it with the woman whose plan it is for accuracy, clarity, and feasibility. Some women may want a copy of it; others may consider it too dangerous should their partner find it. Whether a copy is given to the woman should be her decision; she best knows her situation.

The survival skills strategy plan can be referred to in the group whenever a woman has experienced a violent episode to determine its effectiveness. Its feasibility must be checked since a plan that seemed feasible on paper may not be and may need amending. It can be referred to in each group meeting even if violence has not occurred for the purposes of review and to determine if anything needs changing. Once a woman has begun to think strategically, she may want to alter her plan. And when women hear each other's strategy plan, the new information may affect their own plan.

The survival skills strategy plans can be developed as early as possible, perhaps by the second session of the group. (The first meeting marks the beginning stages of the group and is often used as an introductory session where women get to know one another and the leader.) The reason to introduce strategy plans early in the group process is obvious: women may need to use them in order to survive a battering.

In the second group meeting, the leader said, "Last week, everyone spent time getting to know each other and shared their situations. In this meeting, we want to spend time developing a plan for each of you to help to deal better with your partner and the situation when he gets angry." The women agreed, although some felt doubtful that anything would work. The leader suggested that someone who did feel doubtful might want to begin, and Grace volunteered. The leader asked Grace if people could give suggestions if they wanted to. Grace agreed.

"To begin," said the leader, "are you aware of any signals Thomas sends out when he gets angry?" Grace did not understand, so the leader made some suggestions. "Does he start to sweat, clench his fists, eyes bulge, or anything like that?" One woman said, "My husband's voice changes." Grace acknowledged sometimes that happened—but sometimes it did not. But she noted that at times his voice broke as he began to get angry. The leader wrote down, "Signal: voice breaks sometimes." She asked Grace if she could do something to avoid him when that happens. Again, Grace asked for suggestions. The leader asked if she could make an excuse to leave the room. Grace said she just freezes when that happens. The leader asked if she could make herself act. Since Grace was not sure, it was put down on her strategy sheet, and she was encouraged to try it. The leader wrote, "When Thomas's voice cracks, go to the bathroom if possible."

The leader wondered if someone could come to her aid as the anger escalated. Grace said the only person at home was her 3 year old. The leader asked if she had a sympathetic or friendly neighbor. Grace's quick and guarded response was that no one knew about her and Thomas. The leader asked if she could tell someone. Mary, one of the other women, noted, "There's no shame. My neighbor gets hit too, and I come to her aid when I can, and she comes to mine." The leader asked her how they worked this out. Mary said that when her neighbor heard her husband yelling, she knocked on the door and asked to borrow something or sometimes could even get him to help her lift something too heavy for her. Mary chuckled at the thought of that working, but Grace was not impressed and still did not want to involve anyone else.

The worker asked whether Grace thought that she could do something to deescalate the situation. Grace did not think that was possible; Thomas just kept going once he started, and he wanted her riveted to the spot, "looking at him and listening." The leader asked Grace what she did during this time. Her response was that she tried to appease him. Someone else asked her what would happen if she said and did nothing. Grace did not know but was willing to try. The leader wrote down, "When Thomas's anger escalates, I will say and do nothing."

The leader asked whether it was possible for Grace to get away during an episode of violence. Grace said she could. She had done it twice before. Although she froze at his escalating anger, once he started hitting, her only thought was to get away. She had been able to break free and run after the second blow because he then hesitated and had not grabbed her yet but was swinging freely. "After that, he grabs me, and then I can't move anymore." The leader asked where she could go when she left and whether she will take her 3 year old. She said her mother took her in after a battering. That was a safe place, so it was agreed that her escape plan would read: "When Thomas starts to hit me, after the second blow, I will run out, grab the baby on

DATE_____   NAME_____Grace_____

1. BATTERER'S SIGNALS

Voice breaks sometimes.

2. HOW CAN ANGER BE AVOIDED

   a. When Thomas' voice cracks, go to the bathroom, if possible.
   b. When Thomas' anger escalates, I will say and do nothing.

3. WHERE CAN YOU GO TO BE SAFE?

My mother's house.

4. WHAT FINANCIAL RESOURCES ARE AVAILABLE FOR ESCAPE?

   $10.

5. WHERE WILL YOU KEEP MONEY, ETC?

   a. $10. Always pinned inside of my bra.
   b. Key to my mother's house pinned inside my bra.

6. WHAT IS YOUR PLAN FOR YOUR CHILDREN?

   a. Take the baby with me.
   b. Store a blanket underneath the staircase.

7. ADDITIONAL COMMENTS:

8. STEP-BY-STEP SURVIVAL/ESCAPE PLAN

   a. When Thomas starts to hit me, after the second blow, I will run out, grabbing the baby on the way.
   b. I will store a blanket for the baby underneath the staircase, which I can grab as I'm leaving, if I need it.
   c. I will carry a $10 bill with me at all times, pinned to the inside of my bra.
   d. With transportation money, I will take public transportation to my mother's house.
   e. I will ask my mother for a key that I will also keep pinned to the inside of my bra together with the $10 bill.

Exhibit 4–2 *Survival Skills Strategy Sheet for Women's Groups*

the way. I will store a blanket for the baby underneath the staircase, which I can grab as I'm leaving if I need it. I will carry a $10 bill with me at all times pinned to the inside of my bra. With transportation money, I will take public transportation to my mother's house. I will ask my mother for a key that I will also keep pinned to the inside of my bra together with the $10 bill.'' The leader reviewed her entire survival skills strategy plan and said that next week they would discuss whether she had to use it and how it worked. With that, the leader turned to the group members and said "Next?"

This chapter described the use of group treatment for women remaining in the relationship with the batterer. The rationale for the therapeutic value of groups for these women is well summed up in the following quotation:

> Eventually the oppressed actually come to believe the lies used to justify their oppression. When a person has incorporated in her or her own consciousness the arguments that explain and make legitimate his or her oppression, then mystification and alienation are complete. People will no longer rebel against oppression, but instead blame themselves for it, accept it, and assume that they are the source and reason for their own unhappiness. . . . Being separated from, and unable to communicate with each other is essential to alienation. By ourselves, without the aid of others who are in similar circumstances, we are powerless to think through our problems and do anything about them.[12]

5

Staying

Group Treatment for Batterers

The multimodality approach focuses on two methods for working with batterers: couples therapy and men's groups. (Individual treatment is another approach, although I have not described it in any detail.) The goal of all methods is to eliminate violence. Based on the multimodality approach, the worker and client can choose the method that is best matched to the client's needs. The literature, while mixed, reports that interventions with batterers are effective and favor batterers groups as the preferred method. It has been suggested that a combination of arrest and batterers groups shows the most promise.[1]

The underlying premise for treating batterers is that violent behavior is learned: it is not innate or genetically determined. According to behavioral learning theory, negative behavior that is learned can be unlearned and replaced with more constructive behavior. Defining violence as learned behavior carries with it the notion that the men can change. Not all men who batter, however, can be helped by the method described in this chapter.

RULING OUT BATTERERS WHO CANNOT BENEFIT FROM THE MODEL

Organic Impairment

Some men batter because of organic impairment, which can be identified by psychological and neurological workups.[2] Organic impairments are biochemical disorders. Counseling focusing on the elimination of violence will not be effective in these cases. The primary appropriate intervention in the case of organic disorders usually is medication.

Antisocial Personality Disorder

Persons with an antisocial personality disorder, characterized by a lack of remorse and guilt, frequent lying, and other antisocial behaviors beside violence, cannot be reached through the counseling methods described in this chapter because their illness cannot be easily affected. Their behavior cannot be modified by experience.[3]

In order for batterers to be treated, they must be motivated to change—perhaps as a result of feeling uncomfortable, guilty, or remorseful for harming someone they love.[4] Since one of the major characteristics of the antisocial personality disordered person is that there is an absence of guilt and remorse, there is no motivation for change. Counseling efforts, assuming one could even get such men in, predictably would fail.

Psychotic Disorders

For men diagnosed as psychotic, violence against one's partner is usually part of the psychotic process. Violent behavior cannot be isolated for treatment; rather, the psychosis must be treated. The most appropriate and effective treatment for psychosis usually is psychiatric intervention.

Life-Style Behavior

For some men, the use of violence is a way of life. These men fight with anyone, and violence is pervasive in their lives. In this "subculture of violence," violence is normative.[5] For such men, isolating one aspect of physical abuse (partner abuse) would not be effective. Such men require a total reorientation.

Substance Abusers

A relationship between substance abuse and partner abuse exists, but there is no correlation.[6] Many men who abuse their partners abuse substances; but many men who have no history or usage of substance abuse abuse their partners. Further, even when men are abusing substances, they may batter regardless of their state of sobriety. In assessing whether a substance abuser can benefit from the interventions described here, a diagnosis must be determined. The critical factors to take into consideration are the relationship between the physical abuse and the substance abuse, and the severity of the substance usage.

If domestic violence occurs only when the abuser is using substances, the primary diagnosis is substance abuse. It is assumed that the result of successful treatment will be elimination of the substance abuse and the violence. If there is battering regardless of whether substances are being abused—that is, sometimes battering occurs when the batterer has used substances and sometimes battering occurs in the absence of substance abuse—then an assessment must be made concerning whether the substance abuse would interfere with treatment. Two cases come to mind. In the first case, the substance abuse was a deterrent, and in the other it was not.

In the first case, Bernard came for help upon the urgings of his wife. He was a drinker and cocaine user. He had a very good first session and was motivated to continue, wanting some friends of his to come with their partners also. The second session, he did not show up or call to cancel. He came for the third session but did not remember the content of the first session and was also a half-hour late. He was not honest about whether he had used substances or even whether he was high during the session. He failed to keep his fourth appointment and did not respond to my telephone calls, at home or at work. It became clear that he was nontractable, unreliable, and incapable of making a contract for treatment. His wife continued in treatment alone. Eventually she left him.

In the second case, John's wife said that he used alcohol and cocaine, and John admitted his use. He was in a state of denial concerning the severity of his using drugs. I was unsuccessful about affecting his substance abuse. He came to the sessions regularly, consistently, and promptly, however. He took responsibility for canceling, which occurred very infrequently. At times he came to the session high, and although he did not volunteer this information, he admitted it when I confronted him. During times he was high, his behavior was different: he was somewhat paranoid, less inhibited verbally, and occasionally vague. His behavior and thought processes, though, were still within the range of normal. He was able to engage in the treatment process and carry out treatment plans. Eventually the violence stopped. Throughout this book, a major thesis is the individualizing of each case; this is true for assessing substance abuse as well. There needs to be case-by-case differentials.

For all of these disorders—organic impairment, antisocial personality disorder, psychotic disorder, and life-style behavior—the treatment of choice is not the counseling methods described here. In the case of substance abuse, for example, a careful assessment will determine whether there could be a benefit to treatment for battering.

Who, then, is left for treatment? There are a large percentage of men who function within normal range with the exception of their domestic violence. It is these men who can benefit from the interventions outlined.

MEN WHO CAN BENEFIT FROM COUNSELING

The batterers come from all socioeconomic classes and racial and ethnic backgrounds. Anyone who has not been ruled out by a particular disorder qualifies for treatment. It would be a mistake, however, to expect the men to appear well motivated. Typically they are coerced into treatment in some way: their partner has left them or threatens to take or has taken some action against them, legal or personal. In over a decade of my experience with batterers, not one came to treatment without coercion. (Involuntary treatment based on a court mandate is a separate category and will be discussed later in this chapter.)

It is to be assumed that batterers present an external reason for entering treatment. It is also expected that initially they will justify, rationalize, minimize, and externalize their violent behavior; in other words, they will employ the usual defense mechanisms available to everyone. They may exhibit resistance to change and to the therapeutic process, like any other client. All of this is unimportant. The main criteria for keeping them in treatment are that they come to sessions, that a rapport can be established, and that, within reason, they participate in the therapeutic process. I usually give the treatment process six months before deciding someone is unsuitable. The criterion I use to determine unsuitability is seeing no change in behavior or attitude toward treatment.

THE GROUP

The group is for men who can be roughly categorized as follows.

The first category, men who cannot or will not come for treatment with their partners, may be willing to come for help in the presence of other men. These are men whose life-style includes male bonding and "hanging out with the guys," formally or informally.[7] They may be so alienated from their partners that they could not openly talk about their feelings in the partner's presence. Men whose partners have left them qualify for the men's groups as well.

The second category contains men who are not in sufficient control of their anger to risk couples sessions, which might put the women in jeopardy. Third are men who could benefit from a group experience for all of the reasons one would make a determination for group for any client. Some reasons to consider a group are to combat isolation, for socialization with other men, for male identification and male bonding, and for feedback from peers, which can be more effective than feedback from a worker.[8]

Men can be in more than one modality of treatment simultaneously—for example, in individual and group or couple and group.

GROUP OBJECTIVES

The goals or objectives of a batterers' group are to help men accept responsibility for the violence and eliminate violence.

Prior to the start of the group, each man is interviewed individually by the group leader. A detailed history of the abuse is obtained, and the worst incident is described in detail. If possible, each man writes up his description of the worst incident (not everyone will be capable of putting this into words). The purpose of this step is twofold: the leader needs this information diagnostically, and it is a first step in holding the batterer accountable for his actions. Writing it down formalizes its importance.

MOTIVATING MEN FOR THE GROUP

No batterers in my experience have come forth without external pressure: threats by the partner, ultimatums, advice from personal contacts, strong suggestions from employers, or the actual loss of the partner either because his violence put her in the hospital or she left him. The first contact batterers make with the practitioner, therefore, is because of pressure exerted on the batterer.

A request for help does not necessarily mean a serious intention. In order to motivate batterers to follow through on the initial contact, I have found it helpful to get a commitment from the men to attend the group session one time. Some men admit to the need to stop violence; others deny that they need to change even after making contact with the practitioner. For other men, motivation to change may only occur as a result of participation in the group.

At the initial contact, I do not expect batterers to make a full commitment. The assumption I make is that if they attend one session, they will likely continue. Some drop out after one session or at some point in the future. Two approaches can counteract dropouts. First, in the initial contact, the group is described positively. Men are told that it is a place for men only, where they can talk and share experiences in confidence. The other is that the practitioner running the group be the person to speak to the batterer upon the initial contact rather than an intake worker. The group leader needs to establish a rapport quickly. If a batterer has a positive feeling about the leader, it could sustain him to the first session.

Keith called, inquiring about a men's group for people who have trouble with their anger. Dan, the group leader, spoke to him. Keith said that this did not pertain to him; he was not one of those guys who beat their wives. His wife told him that she would leave him if he did not go for help, so he was calling. She was making a mountain out of a molehill, he said; he called just to keep her quiet.

Dan listened and did not challenge his denials, replying that it might be good for Keith to have a place where he could talk with other guys like himself in private. The group was for men only; they could talk in confidence. Keith seemed interested and asked about the group. Dan told him there were five men who met together weekly at the agency in a private room to talk about what was going on in their relationships and other parts of their lives. Dan described the men, mentioning that all had physically abused their wives. Dan repeated what Keith had said about looking for a group where men have difficulty with anger and wondered if abuse pertained to Keith too. He said that hitting was hard to admit. Dan went on to say that he thought it took a lot for a man to say he abused his wife.

Keith hesitantly admitted to pushing her once in a while and slapping her. When he began to blame her for provoking the violence, Dan interrupted him, telling Keith that he admired him for owning up to that. The men in the group, he said, were learning how to handle anger without violence. He thought it was possible for Keith to learn this too. Keith repeated that he did not think he needed it; it was all his wife's crazy idea. Nevertheless, Dan asked him to come to a meeting and see how he felt about the group. Keith was ambivalent. Dan pushed and suggested that he just come once, and if it was not for him, he could leave, with no hard feelings. Dan asked Keith to come in first to see him alone one time. Keith seemed suspicious, so Dan explained his reasoning. He would like more information about Keith before he came to the group so he could understand him better. Keith still seemed suspicious. Dan reviewed the kind of questions he would ask about his history. Keith finally agreed. Dan said that he would be expecting him, and he did not want him to change his mind. Keith said he would be there. Dan responded with "no excuses," repeating the time and day of the appointment. Keith replied, "I'll be there."

The example demonstrates the worker's use of self in engaging a resistant client. What is effective in motivating each man to attend the group will vary. The main point is that it is common for batterers to be resistant. They may be able to overcome their reluctance to come for help, however, if the initial contact is positive.

THE BEGINNING

Batterers use defense mechanisms to deny their responsibility for violence. The first step toward change, and a necessary one, is helping men to admit their responsibility for abuse. One technique for breaking through resistance about accepting the responsibility is for the behavior to become emotionally uncomfortable. Practitioners can develop discomfort in the men about abusive behavior. This method is described step by step later in this chapter and then again in chapter 6. Although responsibility for violence is the first step, it may not be possible to introduce this topic until after the first group session because of the group members' resistance. Timing and pacing are important; a word said too soon or too late often proves ineffective.

Initially the men's denial of responsibility often dominate the group atmosphere. It is not uncommon for the men to express bravado. They may make negative statements about women in general or about their women, and they may justify their violence.[9] In the beginning phase of the group, the members need to get to know one another and form bonds in order for a group identification to develop that leads to group cohesiveness.[10]

INTRODUCING THE CONCEPT OF RESPONSIBILITY

Batterers often feel victimized themselves. One author has noted that violence occurs when the batterer believes his partner is attacking his sense of self.[11] I have heard men refer over and over again to themes of betrayal and feelings of having been themselves abused by their partners. These batterers usually have little or no empathy, although they feel guilt and remorse. The fact that the men feel betrayed and abused, coupled with their lack of empathy, is frequently the main contributing factor to their abusive behavior. When the group leader introduces the concept that the men are responsible for their abusive actions, these words can easily fall on deaf ears initially and can result in strong resistance by the members sufficient to cause the destruction of the group. Men may not be ready to consider their responsibility for violence until the third or fourth session, although the leader may be able to introduce it in the second session. The leader can use his own discretion regarding when the group will be receptive to hearing this.

The steps described here for helping batterers assume responsibility for their violence and then for eliminating the violence begin with using the visual aid of a film. After several weeks' discussion of the film, the focus moves away from the film to the group members themselves. Other therapeutic aids—role play, for example—are useful as well.

GROUPS USING THERAPEUTIC AIDS

Laying the Foundation

Films are available that are psychoeducational in nature, relatively short, and present situations with battering as their theme, either directly or indirectly. Practitioners can use them to trigger discussion (they are called trigger films) about the issue without focusing directly on individual group members. This technique can raise men's consciousness about the use of violence.

The first step in using trigger films is to focus the discussion on the film content rather than on any of the individuals in the group in order to reduce defensiveness. Batterers who can benefit from treatment know that their behavior is unacceptable, although often they repress this knowledge. At the most elementary level, boys are taught not to beat up girls; beyond that, batterers know battery is against the law. These men love their partners and do not intend physical injury. (There are batterers who may be motivated to do harm to their partners, but that is not the group we are concerned with here.) It is possible that the men's defensiveness is related to how they feel about being abusive without intending it.

Confronting the men's defensive behavior directly can result in strong resistance from them, which ultimately proves counterproductive. Questions about the film content—"What do you think about his behavior?" "What do you see about him [her, them]?" "How did you feel about his saying such and such?"—has the group talking about violence but not about themselves.

It was the second group session, and Tom, the leader, said that he wanted to show a short film and get their reactions. The men liked this idea. There was a lightness in the room. Jim said, "A film. That's more like it!" He was joined by Gregory, who asked if it was a "girlie" film. That evoked laughter, and Leroy said he had a good one home; maybe he would bring it next time. Tony asked if someone was selling popcorn, which caused more laughter. This atmosphere continued for a few minutes into the film, when a hush fell over the room.

The couple in the film started to argue at the dinner table about their son's needing braces on his teeth, and the argument escalated suddenly; the husband threw his glass of soda at his wife, turned over the dinner table, and grabbed his wife by the shoulders, shaking her vigorously while cursing her. Ultimately he punched her in the face, with their child crying hysterically. At this point, the film ended; the men were stone silent.

Tom opened up discussion by asking what they thought of the film. Jim started: "He sure got that bitch good." But Gregory replied, "He didn't have to hit her in front of the kid." Tony chimed in: "He didn't have to hit her at all. All he had to say was, 'Shut up, bitch. We don't have no money for braces.'" None of the members objected to the abusive behavior.

Reality testing, the next step, is useful for eliminating the men's distortions about what they saw in the film that results from their projections. The leader can ask questions pertaining to the facts.

Tom wondered if the problem was solved. The members did not know what he meant. He asked whose idea it was that Stephen, the son, needed braces. Several men said it was the wife's idea. They thought she knew what their finances were, and she should not have asked her husband for something they could not afford and embarrass him. Leroy said, "Yeah. She tried to make him look bad." Tom asked where they got the idea that it was the wife's idea. Jim said, "No. Wait a minute! It was the dentist's idea." Tom agreed and wondered if the husband really wanted Stephen to have crooked teeth. Leroy protested that she should have told him the dentist said so. Tom wanted to know why he did not ask her that. A discussion ensued about whose responsibility it was to communicate clearly—his or hers. Tom said, "While we're talking about the problems they have with each other, anyone see any other problems?" Leroy said that she insulted him; she accused him of being too cheap to care about his child's teeth. Everyone joined in with blaming her. Gregory said, "If my woman talked to me like that, I'd belt her too." That caused a lot of cheers.

Once the film depiction is viewed free from distortion, the leader instructs the group members about what problems interfere with successful solutions; this is the third step. Options for solving the problem without violence occurring can be discussed.

Tom wondered if the husband could have dealt some other way with his wife's insult. No one saw another way; they all agreed she should be slapped down. Tom said he did not agree. He thought that Charlie, the husband in the film, could have told Lillian, his wife in the film, that he did not like her talking to him that way. The men laughed, and Jim mimicked Tom. Tom said that he thought the couple's problems had to do with poor communications in that they did not say what they meant and did not know how to solve problems as a team. He wrote this on the board. Jim asked, "What do you mean by a team?" Tom asked the group if anyone had an idea. Tony said, "The only teams I know about are sports teams." Tom thought that was a good example. He said that couples are a team too. Like sports teams, each member works together on behalf of the whole team—in this case, the family. That was a new idea for the members.

Step 4, attitudinal changes, can be a turning point because it shifts the focus from the objective—discussion about the film—to the subjective—the men themselves. Batterers have been taught traditional values. They see the roles of men and women in very circumscribed, gender-specific ways, and they hold traditional and rigid values about the family.[12] This step focuses on changing attitudes about men and women and their roles and the meaning of family and violence. Last, and perhaps most important, in addition to changing attitudes, the men need to accept the idea that violence is unacceptable. They need to learn alternative ways of behaving when angered. The film can be used as a springboard for discussion. Let us turn to how it was used in the third and fourth group session.

Tom opened up the discussion: "Let me ask you a question. How much respect do you think Charlie and Lillian have for each other?" Ishmil said, "She didn't have much respect for Charlie. A woman should worship her husband, do for him, and be polite." Everyone agreed that Lillian lacked respect. Tom asked, "What about Charlie? Did he respect Lillian?" Jim replied, "Hell, he doesn't have to respect her. He supports her. That's enough." A lone voice said, "I don't know, man. She keeps his house, raises his kid . . ." He was drowned out by protests and the other members' saying that that is what a wife is supposed to do, and it is nothing compared to what the man does. Leroy said one day Maureen, his wife, was sick, and he took care of their 3 year old. He said it was hard work. His remarks were followed by protests from the rest of the group. Tom saw some leverage; two men in the group showed some empathy for Lillian's position. He wondered out loud where it was written that a woman was expected to be grateful for a man's supporting her and that she did not deserve any appreciation or respect. The members looked at Tom as if he was crazy. Puzzled, Tony said, "That's the way it's supposed to be." Ishmil agreed. Tom pressed on and said, "That's the way you were taught; that's not the way it's supposed to be." Jim laughed and said, "OK, I'm going to go home, put on a skirt and apron, shave off my mustache, cook dinner, and say, 'Here's dinner, honey. Just the way you like it.'" Everyone laughed. Tom asked if a man could cook dinner and still be a man. The discussion continued in this vein. At the end of the session, he dared someone, anyone, to do just one of his wife's chores before the next group meeting.

In the fourth session, the focus continued on changing attitudes. Only one man had followed through on Tom's suggestion of doing a chore normally done by his wife.

Mat said, "I did a chore of my wife's. It was hard work." Tom encouraged him to share the details. Mat said he didn't mean to do her work at first. His wife had taken their daughter to the doctor and was stuck on the bus. She called to tell him they would be late. The laundry needed doing. Mat wanted some of his clothes washed for the next day, so he decided he would do it himself. He would take Tom's dare to do his wife's chore. Their six-month-old baby was at home. The baby sitter had left. Mat tried to coordinate separating dark and white laundry, going to the laundry room in their apartment building, doing the wash and taking care of the baby all at the same time. "I was exhausted. My wife came home and I went right to bed. I didn't even wait for dinner. Housework requires a lot of organization. I got to hand it to her for getting it all done."

The film had served the purpose of opening up issues entwined with justifying the use of violence. Suggesting doing a chore normally carried out by the wives was out of role for the men but useful for developing empathy for their wives. This experience can help the men change their views about gender-specific attitudes. At this juncture, the use of the film was abandoned because Tom felt the group was now cohesive. Trust with Tom had been established, and the men had become less defensive. Tom felt the group was ready to talk about themselves.

Accepting responsibility for the violence had not been directly accomplished, but by the fourth session focusing on attitudes was moving the group in that direction. The men first needed to stop objectifying their partners. It is to be expected that discussions about attitudes will take several sessions. Had the men not been ready to talk directly about themselves, the film could have continued to be discussed or other techniques employed.

Another technique is the use of a combination of discussion and the visual aid of illustrative material; this has proved useful to me. Illustrative material can be in the form of assigning television shows about family relations followed by group discussion. Other techniques include didactic material about role formation which can be assigned, read, or described by the leader. Cross-cultural information can illustrate nontraditional roles (according to Western standards), and the use of brief guided imagery can be used where members envision androgynous relationships with their partners.

In using guided imagery, each of the men would be asked to close his eyes and get a picture of himself with his wife. The leader would ask him to imagine doing a chore together that she normally did alone and then, one that he normally did alone; or, to share a decision together that he usually made. A good example of a decision made by him might have to do with finances. The men are asked, either verbally or in writing to describe the image and the scenario. Depending on the level of openness established, the men could be asked how it felt. If the leader feels that this question would cause too much exposure, the exercise ends after describing the scenario.

Developing Violence-Eliminating Strategic Interventions

The next stage of the group focus on how anger can be expressed without resorting to violence in the form of violence-eliminating strategies. The leader helps the men accept full responsibility for the violence by first experiencing their behavior as uncomfortable (ego dystonic). This is not a time for the worker to talk about the injuries to their partners in an attempt to develop empathy. The worker focuses on how using violence makes the men feel about themselves.

One by one, each man is asked to describe how he feels when he hits his partner or following violence. We know that after a battering episode, the men feel remorseful.[13] These feelings of remorse need to be given expression. Men will respond that they feel badly, guilty, did not mean to harm their partners, or something similar. An uncomfortable feeling is the desired response; it enables the worker to comment emphatically about how bad that must feel. Once a batterer is aware of this feeling, he is more motivated to eliminate feeling uncomfortable.

The worker then offers each man the possibility of not feeling discomfort by telling him that the worker can help him to not feel that way ever again. Batterers will usually protest that their partners will provoke them into violence even if they do not want to use violence. This opens the door to helping batterers realize that violence is a chosen response and a choice that they have made by asking if responding with violence to what they perceive as provocative behavior is the only possibility.

If another possibility cannot be thought of, the leader presents alternatives: "Why don't you walk out, tell her you want her to stop, or let her know you can't continue this?" introducing the idea of many ways to respond; violence is only one of several alternatives. Which alternative someone uses is a choice each man makes. Focusing in this way on the batterer's behavior removes the focus from his partner's behavior, further illustrating that he is the subject of this discussion.

The leader, Tom, said that he would begin with Marty and asked how he felt when he hit his wife, Judy. He replied, "Good." Some members laughed. Tom asked what about afterward. Tom admitted he felt guilty. He loved Judy, and when he saw her cry because he hit her, he felt badly. He began to say that she provoked it, though—that she knew what got him mad. Others agreed that their partners provoke the abuse. The leader cut them off: "It must be terrible for you to see your wife in pain as a result of your violence." Marty, eyes downcast, agreed. Tom said that it was a shame he had to feel so uncomfortable. Marty nodded. Tom asked whether he would like to stop feeling that way. Marty asked, "How?" Tom said that he knew a way and would show him. Marty protested that even if he wanted to change, Judy would continue her nagging and harping, which she knew he hated; he would have to hit her again to get her to stop. "Look," said Tom, "is that the only way to deal with her?" Everyone was silent now. Marty said, "What do you mean?" The worker said, "Why don't you walk out when she gets to you or tell her to stop?" Marty said that he never thought of that. Tom wondered why not. He said that maybe Marty wanted to hit her rather than do something else. He continued, "This is a choice you made. There are lots of ways to deal with Judy, but you chose violence. The choice of violence is your responsibility, not anyone else's. It has nothing to do with Judy's behavior."

Using examples from other aspects of the men's lives in which they responded to provocation without violence is another approach. Good examples involve friends or work. The leader can ask what they would have done if a friend, colleague, client, or boss provoked them. Typically the men discuss alternatives to violence, and the worker is able to point out they know more than one method for dealing with provocation. Using violence is a choice. In the following example, the man was being seen individually, but the same principle applies.

Bob was telling the counselor that the last fight he and Barbara had was about his quitting a part-time job sooner than they had agreed to. Barbara was upset at the loss of the extra income months before they had planned; Bob was complaining about the lack of emotional support from Barbara. He felt that Barbara did not understand him and provoked his anger. In reply to why he had decided to quit sooner than the agreed-upon date, Bob explained that there was too much pressure on the job due to management turnover. He was being asked to do much more because he knew more about the business than the new management. They wanted him to work longer hours with more responsibility and for the same pay. When he told his manager that he did not want to do this, the manager pulled rank, telling Bob that Bob would do as he was told with "no lip." This was said in front of other workers, some of them Bob's subordinates. Bob felt exploited, belittled, embarrassed, and angry. He felt "like hauling off and clipping him on the jaw." Instead, he held his tongue and controlled the urge to hit. The counselor commented, "So you do know how to control your desire to hit someone." Bob said, "I had to. I couldn't hit my boss." The counselor pointed out that he made a choice not to hit his boss. He chose to stay in control.

Even if the men exhibit resistance in the form of denial that any alternative to violence exists, the practitioner can challenge this. Remember that these men function within normal range in other aspects of their lives. They have experiences to draw upon where they responded to provocation without violence. Once they and the worker establish that there are situations in their lives where they control violence, the practitioner can place the expectation on the men to control violence with their partners too by saying something like, "I see that you do know how to control your anger. This needs to be applied to your wife too."

Establishing Violence-Eliminating Techniques

Once the batterer accepts responsibility for the violence and recognizes that using violence is making him uncomfortable, violence-eliminating techniques must immediately be established while he is receptive to change. If left for the next session, he will have had an opportunity to build up his resistance again. Motivating the batterer to change and offering change techniques must occur simultaneously. The primary tool the worker uses is the batterer's agreeing to or contracting for no violence.

The batterer is first taught to recognize his angry impulses and then to exercise self-restraint in expressing the anger.

The development of the contract is tailored to the unique situation of each person, taking into account each batterer's personality and life situation. He is expected to participate in writing the contract. He must begin to take responsibility for stopping the violence and be responsible for carrying it out.

The leader determines whether the contract is feasible; in other words, can it be realistically carried out? Then, what has been agreed to is written down in simple and clear steps, with a copy for the worker and batterer, who is asked to memorize the contract. The men are instructed to inform their partners about the contract so the partners know that the men will be responding differently when angry. This also enforces accountability for their actions. If the men tell their partners, the telling makes it official and serves as a commitment to carrying out the contract.

A ritual is used to formalize the contract by the leader having each man's agreement drawn up in the form of a contract with signatures and the date. (A sample contract is shown in Exhibit 6–1, page 114.) The leader signs each contract, and each member signs his own. There is a copy for the leader. The members are instructed to put it someplace where they can easily refer to it should an argument erupt. In the following session, the leader will be asking each member about whether the contract was needed and used. Until the violence is under control, each group session will begin with querying the group about fights and the use of the contract. Discussing violence may take up most of the time in the early groups.

If a member did not follow his contract, the reasons must be discussed to determine if the fault lies in the nature of the contract or with the batterer. If the former applies, the contract must be amended. Sometimes a design on paper that looks feasible is not practicable. If the fault lies with the batterer—he did not follow a feasible contract—there must be consequences. If the partner is willing, she is instructed to take a legal action or leave him. If the partner does not wish to be involved in taking an action, there must be a consequence from the group, such as chastisement, a particular action, such as a hefty fine being paid to his wife, or an apology to his wife in the group's presence in the form of a letter, a tape recorded message or an in-person apology. With one man, the letter of apology caused the batterer to cry when reading it to the group.

Developing Empathy Through Role Play

Role play can be an effective tool for the development of empathy, which most batterers lack regarding abuse to their partners. Batterers often comment on how victimized they feel and that the violence is their response to the victimization; that it is self-defense. In addition to feeling victimized, or perhaps as a consequence, their anger becomes uncontrollable or is used to dominate and control their partner. When angered, they lose their awareness of their partner and how the anger affects the women. A counseling approach that helps them stay aware of their partners' feelings by developing empathy affects the expression of anger and deters it.[14] In role play, the person playing the part can experience the feelings of the role. I do not advise attempting role play initially. It is important for the leader to wait until the members have a moderate degree of comfort with one another before attempting a role play—perhaps the fourth session or so. Topics for role play can center around the kind of family interactions that for these men lead to violence.

The leader begins by setting out the scenario and talking to each participant individually about his role (not in the presence of the other participants in order to create spontaneity). The leader takes control, telling the participants when to begin and end. Finally, the audience analyzes and discusses the situation. The participants share how they felt in the role they were portraying and how others in their roles interacted with them.

Following the role play is a discussion about the topic portrayed and how it relates to each group member. Next, the focus shifts to the men, first on changing attitudes about gender, family, and violence and then on violence-eliminating techniques.

Bob, the leader, said, "Let's do something a little different. Let's get dramatic. I want to try a role play. Let's create a story about a husband and wife and then act it out. We'll make the story realistic. Let's say, Al, the husband, comes home from work. He's tired and frustrated because things didn't go well on the job that day. His wife, Bonnie, was preparing dinner. That's the scenario. I'll tell each player more about his part, and the rest of you will watch."

Before Bob could continue, Lee, a member, said, "Wait a minute. What is this? I'm no actor." Bob reassured Lee that no one had to be an actor and that whoever wanted to could volunteer. Tim said, "Let Jack be the woman. He can really ham it up!" Jack said that he would play any part. Mike teased him and said, "Oh, honey, you're so sexy. Will you go out with me?" Everyone laughed. Bob asked, "Who wants to play the husband?" No one volunteered, and Bob had to coax them. Finally Tim agreed. Bob instructed the rest of the members to listen and watch: "Be the audience, and then we'll talk about what you saw and what you thought about it."

He asked Tim to come outside so he could give him further instructions. He told him he was to play the part of an irritated husband, frustrated and tired, who takes out his feelings on his wife. He feels misunderstood and wants her to pamper him because he had such a hard day. Ultimately they get into a fight. He told Tim to think about how to play this role while he instructed Jack. To Jack he said, "You can sense your husband is in a bad mood, although you don't know why. You think it's something you did wrong, and you feel afraid. You're worried about how bad his mood is going to get. You're worried about a fight." While Jack was thinking about how to play the role, Bob said that he would tell them when to start and end. The seats were rearranged in order to set up a little stage area. Bob asked if Jack and Tim were ready and said, "OK, roll 'em." Jack and Tim proved to be excellent actors. They were convincing and easily got into their roles. At some point, Tim was getting very angry and Bob stopped the role play, telling Tim to calm down. He first asked the audience to talk about what they saw and felt.

Lee said that at first he was angry at Bonnie because he thought she should have been aware that Al was tired and frustrated and needed tender, loving care. Vinny interrupted him: "Yeah. But no matter what she said or did, Al had it in for her." According to Lee, she should have known Al was in a bad mood and should have tried not to bother him. But Tyronne wondered, "What was she supposed to do? Become invisible?" Lee responded, "She could have made an excuse and gone in the other room." José noted, "She was serving him dinner. They were eating! How could she leave?" "I would have left," said Vinnie. "Yeah," Tyronne said, "and what about your dinner? You come home tired and hungry and you would have left! That makes no sense." The members could find no acceptable solution. Puzzled, they turned to the worker. Bob said, "Let's hear from Jack and Tim now. How did each of you feel?"

Tim thought Bonnie was being a "real bitch." She should have seen how tired and frustrated he was and treated him good. He worked hard all day and did not get any gratitude or satisfaction, and she did not appreciate him. She did nothing at her job, and she should have been all over him. Anything she said irritated Tim, and she just kept making things worse and worse until he could not stand it any more. Vinny yelled, "You're wrong, man!" Bob said they could all talk about it soon, but first they should let Tim and Jack finish. Tim said, "I'm finished."

Bob asked Tim how it felt to play Al. Tim shrugged and said, "It was OK." Bob then turned to Jack. Jack said he could see how scary being the wife in that situation could be: "Every way I turned, there was no out. I was stuck. I tried to be nice, and you would just bark at me. Finally, I thought I'd better just shut up." He laughingly said, "At one point, I really thought you were going to belt me!" Vinny said, "He was!" Bob asked how he liked being the wife. Jack shook his head and said, "No way. There was no way out." Bob asked, "Was any of this familiar?" No one responded. He continued, "Maybe the way Jack felt as Bonnie is the way your women feel with you." Tyronne disagreed; "No, I'm not that bad." But Bob challenged this: "No?" Vinny reflected: "Well, sometimes I do come home mad and take it out on Sue." Lee chimed in: "But she must deserve it. I bet she starts it somehow." Vinny hesitated: "Well, I don't know. I used to think it was her fault. Now I'm not so sure. I'm confused." Bob asked if he had an example.

Vinny told a heartfelt story of how he had invited his grandparents to his house for dinner. Although he and Sue had been married two years, Sue and they had never met because they lived in Italy. This was a big moment for Vinny; his grandparents' approval was important to him. He told Sue for weeks how he wanted the house to look, what she should make for dinner, how he would like her to dress. Shortly before the big night, he thought the whole family should come over too, making the dinner for fourteen people rather than four. Bob commented that that was quite a change. Vinny said emphatically, "It was the proper thing to do."

The dinner did not go well. Some of the food was burned. Sue dropped some glasses and spilled wine on the table. Vinny was enraged. After the dinner was over and everyone left, he screamed at Sue, "How could you embarrass me in front of my family and grandparents?" He continued to yell at her and accuse her of making him look bad and ruining the dinner. Everything she said in the way of defense or as an excuse incited his anger. The fight ended by his taking the rest of the wine glasses and breaking them one by one. He then walked out.

Bob asked what he or anyone else thought about this incident. Tyronne shook his head and said there was no cause for his behavior. But Lee disagreed: "Yes, there was. She did embarrass him." Tyronne said, "The girl was nervous!" Vinny looked up, surprised. Bob asked Vinny what he thought about that. Vinny said he never thought about it. Lee said, "That's not true. She tried to make you look bad." Vinny told Lee, "Shut up." Bob asked what others thought. Jack agreed, "She was nervous. All of those people, including your grandparents from Italy. She didn't do anything wrong." Lee said, "She burned the dinner, spilled the wine." Tim said, "You'd spill the wine too in front of all those people." José talked about a similar incident involving himself. He said he felt bad for messing it up. Vinny said he had never thought about this. Bob said, "So here's your wife, catering to your family, trying to help you make a good impression, and what she gets for her efforts is grief." He turned to the other members and wondered how many times each of them had behaved similarly with his partner.

Caution needs to be exercised in using a role play because the person who is enacting a violent role, as in the case of Tim, can get carried away. The loss of control when angered is very familiar, and the ultimate result can be actual loss of control. The leader must stay attuned to that person's emotional state and intercede if necessary. If the person playing the role of the batterer stays in control, it is an indirect way of exercising control and can be addressed during the discussion segment.

Kevin played the role of the batterer. When he reached the point where he was to get angry and start a fight, he yelled at his wife, called her names, and feigned a punch to her arm. During the discussion phase, the leader asked Kevin how he was feeling when he got angry at his wife. Kevin replied, "I was angry, but I didn't feel like hitting her. I only did what you directed me to. I'm only the actor." The leader asked, "You were angry but you didn't want to hit her?" Kevin replied, "No." The leader asked, "If I didn't tell you to hit her, what would you have done instead?" Kevin said he would have told her he was mad and let it go at that. The leader pointed out that Kevin got angry without getting violent. Kevin protested, saying he was only acting. The leader said, "Well, maybe that's what you should do when you're angry at your wife. I think you exercised control."

Exhibit 5–1 lays out the steps and goals of role play.

Topic Discussion

Topic discussion is a psychoeducational method. Initially the leader selects a weekly topic, which the group discusses. Topics cover

Exhibit 5–1   *Role Play*

Steps	*Purpose*
1. Focused discussion with audience "What do you think about . . . " questions "What do you see . . . "questions "What do you feel . . . "questions	Raise consciousness
2. Focused discussion with actors "How did you feel in your role?" "How did you feel about the other person's role?"	Develop empathy
3. Related role play to group members' lives	Develop empathy and change
4. Change attitudes about gender roles, family, violence	Eradicate distructive views Create new options Expand thinking
5. Violence-eliminating strategic interventions	Eliminate violence

the gamut of issues relating to battering—gender issues, role definition, family, anger, stress, and others.

The leader puts a topic on the chalkboard, such as "Being a Man." He asks the members their ideas about the topic, and discussion begins. The role of the leader is to elicit responses. He introduces new ideas that expand the men's thinking and options, broadening their views. Over time, members may be able to suggest topics as well. The leader, however, must always be equipped with topic selections and not rely on the members.

PROCESS GROUPS

In a process group, the worker relies more on the interaction of group members than on therapeutic aids. The strength of the group lies in its individual members' relating to one another with the guidance of the group leader. Group cohesiveness is focused on directly, and it may occur sooner than in groups where therapeutic aids are used. Process groups resemble traditional therapy groups and follow a group therapy framework,[15] but the group stays focused on the topic of battering. The objectives, as in the therapeutic aid groups, are for members to accept responsibility for battering and the elimination of violence.

Session 1 begins the same way as with therapeutic aids groups: the leader states the purpose of the group and defines group protocol; each member is asked to share why he is in the group and what his goals are or what he expects to get out of the group; and the leader listens for whether the goals are feasible and possible.

From the second session on, the therapeutic aids group modality and the process group evidence some diversion. In the process groups, the leader elicits the sharing of feelings from members and encourages members to raise an issue for which they want help. Feedback from other members is expected. The role of the leader is to facilitate communication and interaction among the members, keeping them focused on the purpose of the group: to address issues related to and about violence.

Process groups follow the same pattern as in therapeutic aid groups: initially members are resistant to accepting responsibility for violence, and they employ the usual defensive mechanisms available to us all: rationalization, minimization, denial, externalization, and projection.

The leader must first establish a rapport with the members in order to create a therapeutic alliance, using pacing and timing to break through resistance to change. Once trust is established between the members and the leader, the leader has the opportunity to effect change. At this point the leader can introduce new concepts. Discussions can include confrontation as well as disagreeing with traditionally held values about gender, role definition, and the concept of family.

Once members are receptive to hearing about alternatives to violence, violence-eliminating techniques in the form of a contract can be taught and applied. Usually this occurs between the fourth and fifth sessions, after violence-eliminating strategies are introduced.

All subsequent sessions must begin with a check-in concerning whether there were any episodes where the violence-eliminating techniques needed to be utilized. The leader must carefully and methodically question three things: the event (What happened?), the method (What did the person do?), and the outcome (What was the result?). In my experience, if men adhere to contracts, the result will be that battering will be avoided. If a member did not follow his contract, the reasons are discussed to determine if the fault lies in the nature of the contract or the batterer. The same techniques apply as in therapeutic aids groups. Group members are urged to apply peer pressure.

Some therapists have developed a condition of treatment with batterers called the no-violence contract; essentially, if violence resumes, treatment ends.[16] I see this as a trap for the therapist and coercive to the batterer. Failure to follow the contract—that is, the violence resumes—is a regression and common with anyone who attempts change. This is not a reason to terminate treatment. There must be meaningful consequences when violence occurs, and partners must be safe from harm. Both goals can be accomplished without stopping treatment. A no-violence contract puts the worker in a bind—she or he must carry out the termination once stated—and it does not allow for human error, which, ironically, is similar to how the batterer treats his partner.

According to my definition, a no-violence contract is developed as the result of employing violence-eliminating strategies; it is not a stipulation that if violence resumes, treatment ends. Violence is never acceptable or excusable. A resumption or continuation of it needs to be looked at as an expected relapse of behavior that accompanies change efforts in all therapeutic milieus, regardless of the technique practiced or the problem treated. The group setting affords an added dimension in enhancing efforts at change. Peers can place pressure on member(s) who resist efforts at change once a no-violence group culture is established. The leader is always working to move members forward in terms of both eliminating violence and dealing with the panorama of factors with origins in attitudes and values that set the stage for condoning violence.

Partners should not remain in jeopardy while batterers are learning to control their violence. A safety plan for partners must be developed on the model of the strategy plans outlined in chapter 3. Briefly, this takes into account what she is to do, how she will do it, and what are the resources available to her. The batterer is to know that a plan for his partner's safety has been established, but he should not be apprised of its content. In most states, a professional mental health worker has the duty to protect an intended victim of violence. Practitioners are advised to become informed of the legal requirements.[17]

THE LEADER'S ROLE

The leader is a role model. He or she introduces alternative values, attitudes, and techniques for coping with anger that are violent free. In groups for batterers, the leader should be a man in order to facilitate male bonding and to put the group members at ease. Additionally, resistance and strong defenses, targeted at their partners are clear. It is likely that a woman leader could prove counterproductive in this situation. It might be self-defeating and perhaps even increase members' resistance if they were confronted with a female group leader, for she obviously is "not one of the boys." Nevertheless, there is a place for a woman leader in the men's group. At some point in the group, the members become open to exploring attitudes and values particularly about women; they are more receptive to change. A woman co-leader at this point affords the opportunity for the men to hear and compare the woman's point of view with their own. Additionally, role modeling takes place between the male and female co-leaders. Yalom comments on the benefits of a male-female co-therapy team:

> There is much agreement among clinicians that a male-female co-therapist team may have unique advantages: the image of the group as the primary family may be more strongly evoked. . . . Many patients benefit from the model setting of a male-female pair working together with mutual respect and without the destructive competition, mutual derogation, exploitation, or pervasive sexuality that they too often associate with male-female pairings.[18]

Co-Leader Role Modeling

Once a female co-leader is introduced, there is some flexibility with how she works. A female co-leader can enter the group for limited sessions focusing on attitude and value change. In this situation, the expected outcome may be limited to a dialogue between the members and her, or there could be some role modeling of a healthy partnership. Typically, however, limited sessions usually allow just the minimum, which may or may not be sufficient.

Another option is ongoing male-female co-leadership. After the group members have functioned together as a group for awhile— around the seventh to tenth sessions—it is expected that their defensiveness will decrease and they will become more open. This is the time to introduce a female co-leader. Now the interaction between the two leaders becomes a focal point for change in the members. While the leaders' role continues to be to facilitate the group process, they are also interacting with one another and demonstrating a healthy partnership.

Introducing the Co-Leader

The male leader prepares the group for the female co-leader before she makes her entrance. He presents her in a positive light and processes the feelings about another leader's joining the group and the fact that the co-leader is a woman. Sufficient time must be spent in dealing with members' feelings about this issue. By the time they are ready for a female leader, they have been together a significant and meaningful period of time and have formed a cohesive unit. Any new person entering would encounter a certain amount of mixed feelings from the members, who are now a closed group. Compounding the situation is that the new person is a woman.

The woman joins the group for 20 to 30 minutes initially. She is introduced by the leader, the members introduce themselves to her, and either the leader or the members briefly summarize what they have been talking about. Whether the leader or a member does the filling in depends on who will do it positively. The intent is to draw her in so that she can begin to be viewed by the members as a part of the group. The remaining time is spent with the members' engaging with her. They ask relevant questions so that they can get to know her.

She leaves making an exit statement: "I was glad to meet all of you" or "Thank you for sharing about yourselves," for example. After she leaves the group, the leader asks how the members felt about her. The intent is to prepare the members to be receptive to the introduction of a male-female co-therapy team on an ongoing basis. Any change in format and structure is likely to be met with resistance. The role of the leader here is to be receptive to their feelings and to help them work through any obstacles that will impede the co-therapy situation. This step may take one to three sessions. Before the female leader begins regularly the male leader reminds the members that beginning next session, she will be joining them.

From this point on, leadership will consist of a male-female co-therapy team. In the first session where both leaders are present, the male leader takes the lead to create a transition. He has been leading the group until this point and shares a history with the members. As soon as possible, the female leader should come into the group.

There is also work outside the session that the co-leader team needs to do to enhance their teamwork. Both a pre- and a postsession meeting are valuable.

The Presession Meeting

One-half hour before the group begins, the leaders meet to talk about how each feels working with the other, how each feels at this moment, how each wants the other to help during the session, and the content they need to be aware of and how to focus in the group.

The purpose of the premeeting is to foster communication between leaders and to develop strong teamwork. Unless the two have worked together extensively and are very familiar with each other's style and method, it is expected that they will have to adjust to one another until a productive compatibility can be found so that they are not working at cross-purposes.

The worst outcome of a team situation is that their efforts prove to be counterproductive because they are at cross-purposes or not working together well.

Yalom advises discussion time in order for a good team to develop.[19] Sharing how each is feeling helps each to get to know one another and can aid their work together. For example, if one of them is not up to par that day (tired, not feeling well, or preoccupied), the other can take a more active role, compensating for the weaker leader of that day.

The presession is also used for developing planned intervention strategies. In deciding how to focus the discussion for that group, the leaders may decide that one of them could be more effective than the other for a variety of reasons.

One of the leaders may have more extensive topic knowledge or familiarity. For example, in a discussion of parenting skills, a co-leader who is a parent might take the lead because he or she could interject personal experiences, which aids in bonding and cohesiveness.

Les was complaining that he thinks his wife is making his 3-year-old son Bradley a "momma's boy." He told the group that when Bradley falls, she always comforts him when he cries, and now whenever he falls, Bradley runs to his mother, even when he and Bradley are out playing in the yard and his wife is in the house. Hc wanted Bradley to "take it like a man" and get up as if nothing had happened. He felt his wife was "babying" his son, whom he feared would grow up to be "a cry baby." Robert, the leader said, "You know Les, I remember when my son was about that age, and he did the same thing." Robert went on to say that his son outgrew this phase and talked theoretically about 3 year olds and what can be expected from them developmentally. Robert also shared how he felt when his son ran crying to his mother. Les identified with what Robert was saying. Subsequently Les and Robert would exchange information about their young sons.

Having a better rapport acknowledges human differences. If one leader can reach a member or members more easily because those people just happen to "click" for whatever reason, it will result in less resistance if it is that leader who attempts to get through.

In the presession, the co-leaders, Karen and Robert, talked about Kevin's constant attempts at instigating trouble in the group. The members had not been able to intervene effectively, and the leaders thought it was time he was confronted. They knew this had to be done carefully; they wanted Kevin to receive the feedback openly, and they did not want to lose him. Karen suggested that she take the lead. She had a good relationship with Kevin and thought she could reach him better than Robert could. Robert agreed.

Sometimes one person in a given situation is viewed as having greater authority, which may have to do with age, gender, ethnicity, background, or professional status. It would be foolhardy to ignore the power of these characteristics. They should be used strategically to carry out the desired goal of helping the men to change.

Sal, an Italian immigrant, was the most traditional of all the men in the group; he held fast to his values. He was stubborn about his view that his 18-year-old daughter was not old enough to date, which caused a lot of arguments with his wife. The leaders felt there was a cultural conflict and that he needed educating about American values. It was decided that John, the male leader, would carry the conversation because Sal might not take advice from the female leader, Maria, who was a young woman.

The strategic family therapists have developed a gamut of techniques to counter resistance, such as defiance-based directives or paradoxes which are dependent upon clients defying directions. One example would be to restrain clients from changing; another follows in the illustrated example. The reader is advised to look at the literature on strategic family therapy by such authors as Peggy Papp and Cloe Madanes.[20] Now allow me to illustrate the use of this technique:

The two leaders noticed that every time an intervention was made with Gil, he did the exact opposite. They decided that they needed to confuse him so that he could not tell clearly what the intervention meant and therefore would not be able to oppose it.

Although the leaders use the presession to prepare how they want to focus the group that day, the unexpected is expected, calling for flexibility and spontaneity. Discussion about where to focus in the presession is meant only as a guideline for the leaders to enable them to work in consort.

The Postsession Meeting

Following the end of the group, the leaders need to evaluate how the session went, share how they worked together, including the negative and the positive, and decide on a direction for the next session.

Any partnership takes work. If the leaders are to develop a good working relationship, they must evaluate the progress of the group and also of each other. Co-therapists can provide important feedback to one another about each other's behavior.[21]

It had been a very tough session. The leaders had to work hard to maintain group cohesiveness after the members found out that the agency director had one of the men arrested when he burst into the offices unannounced, drunk and violent. The men were angry at the agency and discouraged about the possibilities of progress. They were blaming everyone but Howard (the drunk group member) for the problem. While they came to the group, they came only to "tell off" the leaders, John and Maria. The leaders worked diligently to hold the group together, and they were successful.

In the postsession, they evaluated and analyzed what had happened and congratulated themselves for their good work. John, however, had noticed that Maria had hung back at the most volatile moments and, he felt, had tried to cut off the members' angry expressions, particularly at the director. Maria felt that they needed to remember that anger easily leads to violence with these men; she thought she was monitoring the men properly. John disagreed; if the men were not given a therapeutic outlet for the expression of anger they felt, he said, they would carry it with them, misdirect it, and perhaps displace it on to their partners. He felt the group setting was the appropriate place and that he and Maria had the control. Maria thought that John was encouraging their anger against the director, in particular because of a falling out that John had had with him. Maria and John had to determine whether their own feelings were getting in the way of the group process.

Openness and honesty between the leaders lays the groundwork for positive role modeling. The leaders are dealing with men who have had destructive relationships with women. As the men learn how to have positive relationships with women, the role modeling the leaders will do will prove instructive. It cannot be performed; it must be sincere.

The Leader as Role Model

No two people think exactly alike all the time or at all, so it is likely, and expected, that one leader will go off in a direction that the other leader does not understand or agree with. In these circumstances, the choices are to remain passive and uninvolved, attempt to change the direction, or bring these feelings out in the open. My belief is that the last is most beneficial. People are allowed to disagree: "Therapist disagreement may contribute greatly to therapy."[22] In fact, batterers need to learn this and see it work in a group. Disagreeing should be raised noncritically, and the leaders should have a dialogue about it.

Karen raised the issue about who watches the kids on a Sunday. But the group had been talking about problems at work, and Robert, the other leader, did not know where she was going: "Karen, I'm not following you. I don't understand your question." Karen told him, in front of the members, that she thought problems at work and how they felt about how they spent their Sundays were related. She had a hunch that some of their wives wanted them to watch or be involved with the kids on Sunday. As a wife and mother, she felt that way herself. Robert said that he could see what she meant.

In another instance, Robert and Karen disagreed in the group:

Karen said that she had to say something about what the members were saying. She felt there should be complete honesty in a relationship, with no holding back and no secrets. One of the members challenged this, feeling there were certain circumstances where it was best not to reveal all and gave examples. Karen was adamant about her position, but Robert said he did not agree with her. He felt that a relationship could be good and close and there could still be holdbacks. The two of them discussed why they felt as they did, and the members listened. It was clear that they could not agree. They both concluded that they disagreed and moved on to something else.

In both instances, what the members saw was invaluable to their learning process: two adults, one man and one woman, in a partnership, who shared different, and in the last example opposing views, and they were able to talk without the situation's becoming destructive or affecting their relationship negatively. No verbal message could have conveyed as well what the members actually saw demonstrated. They may carry this to their own experience; some will even replicate it.

COURT-MANDATED BATTERERS

Involuntary clients are those who have been arrested for battering and are remanded to counseling by the court. These clients are often more resistant to treatment than the non–court mandated or "voluntary" client. The batterer feels that he is being forced or coerced into treatment, and he may refuse to become engaged in the therapeutic process or direct hostility toward the worker, (Not every batterer who is court mandated is resistant. For some men, the feelings evoked as a result of being court mandated will result in motivation to do well and conquer their violence.) Usually if the latter is addressed first, it helps the former.

The court-mandated batterer often identifies the worker with the criminal justice system, seeing him or her as an instrument of the law and part of the system that forced him into treatment. An effective approach is to tell him the reality: "This is neither your nor my choice; you did not choose to come, and I did not choose to have you come." The purpose of this is twofold: it is the truth, and it should help to align the two of you rather than keep you in opposition because you both are in the same boat. A reaching out should follow with the statement that you both should make the best of the situation and use it productively.

A belligerent Gerald entered Carlos's office, jerked out the chair, and sat down, staring into space. He did not respond to the worker's salutation. Carlos told him they would be meeting weekly. Before he could proceed further, Gerald exploded, saying he did not choose to come here, and he does not believe in any of this "faggot bullshit talk." Carlos countered, "I didn't choose for you to come here either. I didn't choose to work with you anymore than you did, so we're both in the same boat. This could be easy or hard. How about if we both make the best of it."

Another approach is less direct and confrontational: negotiating with the court that mandated clients have to show up only once. The leaders then rely on their skill at engaging the resistant client. Not forcing clients to come continuously helps break through the resistance precisely because the client was not coerced. At the intake meeting, the client is told that if he comes once, a letter will be written to the court saying he came. The effect this seems to have is to dilute resistance.[23]

Involuntary status is an initial hindrance, but it is also an asset because it gives the worker leverage. In any therapeutic process, many clients do not complete treatment and drop out. Batterers usually enter treatment after a crisis (usually a battering episode), and they are prone to terminate treatment shortly after the crisis subsides, usually during the honeymoon or remorse period. A court-mandated client gives the worker leverage for continued treatment because the worker has the power to report that the batterer dropped out of treatment against recommendation. The worker can also use this leverage during treatment to stimulate motivation.

Regardless of the approach used to address the resistance when someone is court mandated, effective treatment can facilitate continued contact and decrease resistance. If the client experiences treatment as effective and helpful, it often has the effect of diluting his resistance.

Treating battering is difficult. Working with the batterer is especially hard because of the feelings it evokes for the worker about people who are violent and the intensity of the work. But men who batter can be treated. A second method for treating men who batter, couples counseling, follows in the next chapter.

6

Staying

Conjoint Therapy—A Radical Approach to the Treatment of Battering

At seven o'clock in the morning, there was a call on my tape machine from a man who identified himself by name, said that he just beat up his wife and that it was urgent that he come in immediately. When I returned his call, he told me that he had called other services for battering too. He wanted to stop the violence. He was aware that it was his responsibility, and he knew that he needed help in learning how to curb his violent tendencies. His wife had left and said she would not return until he went for help. He was calling me because he and his wife wanted to come in together. The other services he called did not offer that option.

Walker states that 50 percent of all women who stay in a shelter more than one week never return to their violent partners,[1] which leaves another 50 percent who do return. Additionally, many women never enter a shelter. Although many women remain with their partners for the reasons described in chapter 2, some stay because of a belief that if they obtain help, the relationship might have a chance to improve.

There are many realistic reasons for couples to continue the relationship. We are a nation who, for the most part, pair for romantic love reasons. The high rate of divorce notwithstanding, we still irrationally and fervently believe that love conquers all. Anthropologist Hervé Varenne, studying American society, captured the essence of Americans' belief about love: "Love is the domain par excellence of subjectivity, the unconscious, the nonscientific: it cannot, it must not be possible to explain 'why' so-and-so fell in love with so-and-so. A favored comment is one that stresses the illogical character of the choices, the fact that the protagonists had little influence on themselves and that they started loving the other without realizing what was happening to them 'until it was too late.' "[2] This belief that love will overcome great odds is woven into the fabric of our society. When two people decide to settle down together and share a life, it is hard to give that up.

Batterers do not batter all the time. When a man is being loving and caring, it is hard for the partners to give up their couple status and membership and family ties. In this society, with its emphasis on family as the cornerstone of American life, ending a love relationship and a family relationship is not done lightly or readily.

A large percentage of couples wish to salvage a violent relationship rather than terminate it.

Treatment for batterers alone is one method of dealing with those who can benefit from help; conjoint treatment when it is safe is another, and I often find it is the preferred treatment when battering is mild to moderate. Working with the batterer without his mate excludes her from getting help for the effects the abuse has had on her and from participation with her partner in a safe environment.[3] This last point is the core underlying reason for seeing a batterer and partner together. In adult relationships, both parties form a partnership in which they bond and function as a team on behalf of each other. They share with one another their joy and their sorrow, their good times and hard times, their fears, their needs, their wants, their hopes.

Battering partnerships do not achieve this state; there is little or no consistent positive bonding and constructive teamwork. They are not friends but enemies, and their home is not a haven but a war zone. Each of them stays on the alert for attack, and each feels a need for an arsenal to defend against the other. They feel they have been betrayed and victimized by the other. In treating them conjointly, the opportunity to learn how to achieve a positive adult partnership presents itself. These couples need to work cooperatively together, they need to listen to each other's hurts, desires, and dreams, and they need to understand and develop empathy for one another.

The men tend to lack awareness of the effects of their violence on their partners.[4] The men themselves feel victimized and in their blurred vision do not realize that they are the victimizers. In the monitoring environment of the helper's office, they can learn empathy and find out how to eliminate violence.

CONJOINT OR SEPARATE SESSIONS?

Should couples be treated conjointly or separately?[5] In the conjoint modality, a concern is that the woman is not free to say what is really in her heart or on her mind because of her fear of and intimidation by her partner. But her withholding is detrimental to her and the treatment because the worker misses important information. A further concern is that information she reveals may anger her partner, inciting another violent episode. Another point of view is that the problem of violence is his, and he should solve it without her assistance; seeing the couple together implies that they have a mutual problem to be solved and that equality exists between them.

Clearly the batterer is physically stronger and more powerful than his female partner; they are not equal. It is also clear that the violence is the sole responsibility of the batterer. This is said explicitly, unequivocally, and clearly to the batterer and in the battered woman's presence. Holding the batterer solely responsible for the battering and including the battered women in sessions with the batterer are not mutually exclusive. I do not disagree with the feminist perspective that men and women are not equal, but from a treatment perspective, my focus must be on treating the clients who want the violence to stop, the relationship to be saved, and to be seen as a couple. Whatever are her reasons, the woman's request is to remain in the relationship but without the violence. If both parties are willing to work on that problem together, the couple can be seen together. Seeing the couple together enables the practitioner to work with the entire system rather than just half of it, as occurs when seeing the batterers and battered women separately. Further, seeing the couple conjointly is consistent with a family systems orientation whose basic tenet is that family members form a system with each person's actions affecting every other person in the family (system). The family's operations can be understood by seeing the family members as a unit.

A solution to the problem of women not feeling free to speak openly is to hold both individual and conjoint sessions. Sometimes it is appropriate and relevant to meet with one partner individually; not everything in a person's past or present life or feelings needs to be shared with the other, although it may be necessary for the worker to know certain information in order to provide good treatment (for example, whether one party really wants to end the relationship but needs help in carrying that out or if there is severe pathology in one partner that the other cannot reveal in the pathological partner's presence).

When the batterer has not yet gained sufficient control over his violent behavior, it is more suitable to work with him and his partner separately before setting up conjoint sessions. Conjoint sessions are held only when they do not place the woman in danger. Concerns about worker neutrality and the formation of coalitions between worker and a partner can be dealt with by the worker's awareness of their occurrence and the balancing of individual and conjoint sessions; that is, each party can have a similar number of individual sessions. When arranging an individual session, both parties should be questioned concerning his or her feelings about this, and concerns should be worked through. If separate and conjoint sessions are mixed throughout a couple's treatment, the detrimental possibilities are minimum.

DETERMINING SUITABILITY

Not all batterers are suitable for the treatments described in this book. The worker needs to assess whether a batterer can benefit from a counseling approach or some other method of intervention. The assessment techniques set out in chapter 5 that are used to determine suitability for treating batterers by the methods set forth in this book need to be applied in determining suitability for couples treatment, with the addition of several other criteria.

A considerable amount of time—10 to 30 minutes—during the initial contact is needed in order to determine suitability for couples work. This initial contact usually is by telephone and usually by the victim. The first question to ask after she presents her problem is what her ideal situation would be. The worker might say, "If you could have things any way you wanted them in this relationship, what would you ideally like?" Often the woman protests that what she would like is not possible, but the worker needs to persevere. Usually the woman says that she would like to remain in the relationship but without the battering. After laying out all of her options (legal intervention, safe havens, separation/divorce, separate counseling

for her either in women's groups or individually) and discussing each
one separately, the worker can suggest that her partner come in. The
options concerning cessation of batterer violence are batterers'
groups, couples and conjoint treatment, and a multiple couples
group. I point out to women that the battering cannot be stopped
without the batterer's being treated. It is clear that her attempts to
get him to stop have not been effective, nor have anyone else's.

Getting him in is her job for several reasons, both practical and
therapeutic. On the practical side, she knows him best. He is her
partner, and she has had experience with him. More important than
the practical is the therapeutic. By indicating to her that she be the
one to invite him to the sessions, the worker is using a strategy of
empowerment and shifting the system. It is empowering that the
worker thinks she is not helpless and can be effective.

It needs to be determined whether she can discuss with him that
she has called about counseling, and caution must be taken in
advising that she talk to him about seeking help. There are many
victims of domestic violence who are not allowed to use the
telephone, for example, or tell anyone about the abuse. She is to be
taken at face value if she responds that she cannot mention to him
this call. If this is the case, a method of treatment other than his
receiving help should be suggested (a women's shelter, a women's
group, or an order of protection, for example). In order to avoid any
illusions that the battering will stop without his participation, she
should be informed that counseling methods that exclude him from
treatment will not stop the violence. If, however, she indicates that
she can mention her call, she needs to choose between suggesting he
be seen with or without her. A discussion concerning the advantages
and disadvantages of each can take place.

If the woman decides to be seen with her partner, I recommend
that it be assessed whether the couple begins conjointly or not. Her
level of comfort, as well as the worker's assessment of the degree of
danger, is a good guide.

Psychosocial information and an extensive history of the abuse
must be taken initially in individual sessions. The history of abuse is
obtained from both parties. Each partner describes in detail the
worst incident, which is written down by the worker or the client.
Describing the worst incident has the effect of concretizing its
seriousness.

The individual sessions also help in assessing whether the couple is
suitable for conjoint counseling or whether they need to be seen

separately. The worker questions each partner as to whether each wants to be seen conjointly, and a safety plan is developed for the woman. The batterer is informed that a safety plan has been developed, including use of legal resources, so that he understands that a resumption of violence will have consequences.

Whether the batterer is treated conjointly or separately, the first goal of the treatment is to eliminate violence. The succeeding goals relate to the marital relationship, using techniques employed in couples and family therapy.

FAMILY SYSTEMS THERAPY

Conjoint treatment as described in my model draws on family systems therapy techniques combined with violence-eliminating strategies. Family therapy techniques form the framework for this method. A knowledge of family therapy, however, is not in itself sufficient for treating couples where violence is present. In addition, one must be equipped with a cadre of violence-eliminating strategies used in concert with family therapy techniques.

In family therapy, the emphasis shifts from an individual to a family focus. That is, the family, not the individual, is identified as the patient or problem. According to the family therapy systems theory work of Jay Haley, the reasons for this shift in focus have to do with the fact that families have a history and a future together.[6]

Families follow organized ways of behaving together, and each person has a place in a family's hierarchy; some above and some below the others. Everyone helps to maintain this hierarchy, and the family members step in to restore the hierarchy when someone steps out of order, a process often referred to as maintaining the homeostasis. Roles have been established, and every member has a relationship to every other member. One person's stepping out of order affects everyone else. In unhealthy families, the hierarchy needs to be shifted, but there is a resistance to change because of comfort with the familiar, even if it is dysfunctional. The resistance to change is not conscious or deliberate, however.

In families with problems, the hierarchy is, in Haley's parlance, "confused." Roles are unclear, and one member at one level of the hierarchy may form a coalition against a peer with a member at another level of the hierarchy. In couples therapy when violence is present, it is common for each partner to try to form a secret coalition with the worker. The task for the worker is not to side consistently with any one member against another, which forms another coalition. The worker must join in different coalitions at different times while ultimately not siding with anyone against anyone else. The need to maintain a neutral position is critical when treating couples of violence. (Being neutral does not mean to be cold or unfeeling.) These couples are enemies living in a war zone; as part of their arsenal, they are seeking to get the worker to side with one against the other. Although it is natural to side with the obviously injured party, the worker must resist this tendency. The batterer feels he is wrong, and the worker's siding with the woman confirms that feeling. A batterer cannot lend himself to treatment if he feels the worker is against him.

The worker can map out the hierarchy by observing the sequences that occur in a family; for example, when A tells B to do something, B consistently complies. The conclusion is that A is higher in the hierarchy than B. Sequences have a repetitive and cyclical nature; that the same pattern happens every time in the same way. For example, every time Susan tries to discuss how their money is being spent, it leads to an escalating argument, culminating in Jim's becoming violent, which ends the discussion. Because it has been unresolved, the issue arises again. Jim gets angry again and escalates to violence, which ends the discussion—and the cycle begins again. The task for the worker is to change the sequence by intervening in such a way that the pattern cannot continue.

In couples with violence present, helping the batterer agree to control his anger rather than let it explode into violence is a major step in breaking the pattern of violence. Teaching couples when to table a discussion because the topic becomes too volatile intervenes in the repetitive and cyclical sequence. In addition, families collude to sabotage efforts at change in the service of maintaining the unconscious need for homeostasis. With couples where violence is present, the collusion often takes the form of broken agreements in the form of what I am calling a contract or not showing up for appointments. Workers need to take an active role in reviewing contracts and directing that they be enforced, as well as pursuing couples who have missed appointments.

Understanding that families form hierarchies that they are reluctant to change, that change will be resisted through collusions and sabotage in order to maintain homeostasis, that families form coalitions and experience sequences that are repetitive and cyclical in nature, and that the task of the worker is to maintain neutrality and intervene in the dysfunctional patterns of behavior forms a foundation of how to approach fighting families.

TECHNIQUES FOR TREATING COUPLES

Violence-eliminating strategic interventions must be melded with family therapy techniques in order to treat couples. These cognitive-behavioral-communications strategies include crisis intervention, treating aggression and homework assignments.

Crisis Intervention

Treating violence means intervening in crises; it is to be employed upon any threat of violence or if battering has occurred. The goal of the intervention is to solve the presenting problem (the crisis) through immediate response, focusing on the presenting problem with a determination of psychological and physical safety, and issuing a directive that results in a solution to the problem.

An anxious and panicked Mary called as directed to say that Fred was very angry, and she was afraid he would become violent. He had been threatening her and the family. In the background, I could hear Fred throwing furniture; Mary was yelling at him to stop, which fueled his anger. I directed Mary to stop telling him to stop because it was making him angrier and to tell Fred that I wanted to speak to him. He refused. I told her to tell him that he promised to talk to me should he feel out of control. It took three tries, but he finally came to the telephone.

He started the conversation by calling Mary a bitch and telling me in a loud voice how she made him get angry at her. I directed him to calm down, stop talking, and listen. I reminded him of his contract. He said he did not give a damn about any contract and that she had provoked him. I interrupted, saying it did not matter what his reasons were or who provoked what. What counted was that he needed to control his anger so that she did not leave him, the police would not be called, and he did not feel badly after the episode was over. I told him if he refrained from hitting her, he would feel better about himself, and that was the goal of the counseling. Did he remember that? He said, "Yes, but . . ." several times, with my interrupting him every time reminding him that he made a deal to follow the contract, and that is what he had to do now. The issue was too hot for them to deal with alone and needed to be discussed in a session. He finally agreed. I asked him to repeat what his contract said and what he had to do. I directed him to put Mary on the telephone so that I could tell her what he and I agreed to.

Mary got on the telephone; she was agitated and sobbing, so I suggested some relaxation techniques. I informed her about what had transpired between Fred and myself and told her that they were not to talk about the issue until the session because it was too volatile for them. I reminded her that she had a part to play in Fred's contract. He was to leave the house for an hour. She was to let him go and not question him about where he went when he returned. She agreed. I asked if she felt she was OK. She still felt scared. I asked her if she wanted to visit her friend, as we agreed she would do if she felt too shaken. She thought that was a good idea.

Family violence cases always have a critical aspect to them because of the potential for violence. When working with the couples, treating the aggression is the main objective, but in that process, it is necessary to intervene in a crisis. The goal of the intervention is to stop violence from occurring by influencing the systemic behavior—a different goal than is used when not treating the batterer.

Couples presenting with violence need an opportunity to vent, complain, and even fight in the presence of the worker. Most of them have bottled feelings and need an opportunity for outpouring in a safe environment. Initially, they spill their feelings in counseling sessions. Listening to the fights demonstrates to the couple worker comfort with anger; more important, it demonstrates for the worker their fighting patterns and the issues they fight about. Fighting for too many sessions, however, repeats their patterns and serves to maintain homeostasis.[7] Workers should intervene in the fight after the patterns and issues are established for the worker and direct them to stop fighting, since it is nonproductive. I attempt to allow fighting to occur only in the initial session. Under no circumstances should it continue later than the third session, with the worker moving the case along toward the cessation of violence.

Treating Aggression

Eliminating the violence is the reason to treat the aggression and is accomplished with several procedures. Violence cannot be eliminated without the batterer's motivation. It can be assumed that if a batterer voluntarily enters treatment, he wants to change, but because of his psychological defenses and his fear that change is impossible, the worker needs to increase and make explicit his motivation. Implicit to motivation is the batterer's assuming responsibility for the battering.

Batterer Responsibility

Most batterers, whether treated with or without their partners, initially deny that battering is their responsibility or that they see reason to stop. They may say, "She makes me do it because she provokes me," "Knocking a woman around once in a while teaches her who's boss," or "I only gave her a little slap."

In the face of the man's denials, rationalizations, minimizations, and externalizations, workers need to remember that batterers can and do change and they must understand defense mechanisms. In spite of the batterer's initial lack of admission that he alone is responsible for the battering or that he needs to change that behavior, the worker proceeds on good faith and the professional knowledge that if someone comes in for treatment voluntarily, he wants to be there.

The first step is focusing on having him acknowledge that he alone is responsible for the battering. When a batterer tells me that he is not responsible (usually because she provokes him), I often ask if he thinks other partners are provocative too. Then I wonder if he thinks all men who have provocative partners respond with violence. This is one root to his seeing his responsibility for violence. If he thinks that other men may respond to provoking partners differently, he is faced with understanding why he does not. If he does say that all men who are provoked by their partners respond with violence, I question whether he can think of another way to respond, even to the point of making suggestions ("Why don't you just walk out?" "Why don't you tell her you want her to stop provoking you?") in an attempt to help him see that the way he responds is his choice. The object of this initial step is to engage the batterer in order to develop a therapeutic rapport that will eventually lead to a therapeutic alliance. If a batterer acknowledges the domestic violence is his responsibility, then a dent has been made in his defensive armour, and he is open to hear about his need to change.

The second step deals with asking him how he feels when he hits her. Many people cannot identify their feelings, and sometimes they resist talking about feelings. But many batterers feel badly and guilty for their violent behavior or secretly wonder if they are crazy. At the most superficial level, most men have been taught as children that boys do not fight with girls. For men who cannot articulate their feelings, I identify these feelings for them by saying something like, "I suspect you feel bad when you hit Joan." If I receive no verbal protest, including silence, which I interpret as consent, I assume that he agrees with me. Once a batterer admits that he feels badly about hitting his partner, he experiences his behavior as ego dystonic.

The third step in treating aggression is to develop a violence-eliminating contract. The contract is set up along lines that are both cognitive and behavioral and is aimed at redirecting violent behavior into nonviolent channels.

Contracts

The contract or agreement is made with the batterer's participation and a cooperative effort by the partner. Its purpose is to teach self-control by delaying the urge to respond to anger with violent aggression. His partner's participation enhances bonding and develops teamwork. When they are successful in carrying out the contract, it is empowering and reinforcing. The procedure is as follows:

RECOGNIZING THE SIGNALS

1. Teach the batterer to recognize the cues that signal when anger will escalate to violence—for example, sweaty palms, stomach knotting, increased heartbeat, lightheadedness, dizziness, or tension in various body parts. His feeling the kind of anger that leads to violence signals him to use the contract. If he cannot identify any cues, then whenever he gets angry, he will need to employ the contract.

2. Examine what he can do to control his explosive anger—for example, take a walk, jog, go into another room, beat his fists on pillows, or vigorously play a sport. The batterer must give the final sanction concerning what will work. It has to be his decision drawn from what is normal and feasible in his life frame. Moreover, his participation in deciding alternative behavior to violence conveys his responsibility for change, which is an important shift. (The worker has to monitor its feasibility; a car ride to cool off if he has a car that does not work properly would probably increase his anger rather than decrease it.)

3. Determine exactly how much time is needed to calm down. It is necessary to be explicit and specific. The specificity builds an external structure that will eventually be internalized.

BONDING

4. Involve the partner in a cooperative execution of the contract. Cooperating in a mutual effort for the benefit of each member of the couple and the relationship teaches teamwork and provides an opportunity for bonding. Of secondary benefit, it changes the victim-assailant roles. If she participates and has influence, then her victim status changes. It is empowering for her to be of constructive assistance. During the development of the contract, she has input into whether she can agree to the terms of it. If she finds his suggestions not feasible for her, then the two of them work on it until they reach a mutual decision. The objective is to avoid violence; it supersedes other objectives until successful.

DIRECTIVES

5. Settle on a limited number of times that the couple attempts to resume a discussion that escalates to violent anger; my suggestion is no more than three times. If they cannot have the discussion without escalating anger, then the topic is considered too volatile and they are directed to table it until the session with the worker. If a volatile topic triggers violent anger, the batterer is directed to employ the contract as soon as he feels angry.

6. Review what has been agreed upon to uncover and correct any errors in the contract.

7. Have each member of the couple repeat the contract as many times as necessary until it is repeated correctly. An angry batterer is out of control. He has not been able to draw on inner resources to

contain his anger; therefore, the worker must provide the structure externally, which will eventually be internalized. Give a copy of the contract to each partner, with instructions to put it in a place where there is ready access and to review it regularly. (The refrigerator door is a good spot.)

In the next and subsequent sessions, the worker reviews what transpired during the week and whether the contract was used, as well as the outcome (Did it work?). It is to be expected that the contract will have been broken initially. If violence occurred, the consequences for the resumption of the violence must be put into effect. The worker examines with the couple why the contract was not used. Is the fault with the couple or the contract? If the former, it must be repeated that the contract is to be used and when. If the problem is the terms of the contract, the terms need to be altered. Sometimes what appears to be a feasible contract on paper is not feasible in reality. Any new contract terms are repeated by the worker, then the batterer, and then his partner until it is perfect, and then it is written down. If the old contract is used, each partner repeats the contract again.

At each session, the worker and couple review their days between the sessions, noting any uses of the contract. A resumption or continuation of violence is treated as regression or resistance and never results in termination of treatment until it is clear to a worker that the batterer cannot respond to this method.

Sondra and John came in together. Sondra was verbal and related all the fights they got into, noting the insignificance of the subjects they argued over and how ashamed she was to admit to them. John was silent, squirming in his seat and looking very uncomfortable. When he did speak, he criticized Sondra for hanging out their dirty laundry in public, saying that these things were nobody's business. The two of them got into an argument, which I watched and listened to for awhile before directing them to stop.

I turned to John and asked him how he felt when he hit Sondra. In a defensive tone, he said that she deserved it and that I could see how she bad-mouths him and starts arguments. He turned to Sondra, and they began to argue again, which I stopped. I again asked John how he felt when he hit Sondra. He told me he would not have to do it if she did not provoke him. I asked him if he knew what it made him feel, leaving aside whether she deserved it. He looked blank and said he did not know what I meant. I asked how he felt about what he had done when the fight was over and he was no longer angry. He said he did not like it. He loved Sondra and did not want to hurt her. He turned to her and asked, "Why do you make me do it?" Sondra was about to answer, but I interrupted her, again addressing John. I said that if he did not like hitting her, I thought it probably made him feel badly about himself. Sheepishly, he turned his head away and was silent. I pressed further, saying I could tell he felt badly and that I thought he would want to stop so that he did not feel that way. He hesitantly said that if she left him alone, he would stop. I told him I thought it had nothing to do with what she did but that he had to think about how he could feel better.

In the next session, Sondra and John came in angry. I could tell by their demeanor and their faces. They told me that after the session, things were better for a few days, but then the violence started again. Each blamed the other for the fight starting. I stopped them, saying they did not have to come here to fight; they did that very well by themselves. I thought we needed to find ways for conflicts not to get out of control. I reminded John of what he said the last session about not liking himself after he hit Sondra. He had forgotten, but I insisted that he remember. I also wondered if he thought that other men had wives who provoke. He thought all women were like that and laughingly said, "It's their nature to be pain in the butts to their men." I wondered if he thought that all men responded as he did—by hitting their women when they got like that. He said his friend just walks out of the house, and that is why his friend is over at his (John's) house so much. I pointed out that his friend dealt with his wife's provocations by walking out of the house and followed with, "So there's more than one way to respond." I thought responding by hitting Sondra was a choice on his part. He looked confused. I repeated the example of his friend and said his friend left the house rather than hit his wife. He said he was not going to go out into the cold and rain every time Sondra annoyed him. I said, "Maybe not," but the fact that he hit her when she annoyed him was his choosing, his responsibility. He could tell her to be quiet, ignore her, go into another room . . . any number of other things, but instead he hit her. I thought that if he felt badly about hitting her, maybe he could find another way—for his sake, not necessarily her's—so he did not have to feel badly so much of the time. I asked him to think about that and what he could do instead for next time. I instructed Sondra not to help him figure out alternatives.

The third session I began by asking John if he thought about what we had talked about last time. He had not. He said he worked a lot of overtime this week and got home dead tired and just went to bed. I suggested he think about alternatives to hitting Sondra now, in the session. He did not know what he could do. Sondra started to make a suggestion, but I stopped her, saying, "Let's hear from John first." He thought maybe he could watch television when he got annoyed at Sondra. I asked how that would help; he did not know. Sondra said that was one of the things that started arguments: either the television was too loud, or they fought over what to watch. I ruled that out and asked John to think of something else, but he could not.

I remembered he had said his friend left the house and that he did not want to do that. I wondered, though, if he could go into another room until he cooled off. He said, "She'd only follow me and keep up her mouthing off." I wondered if it would work if she did not follow him. He thought it might. I asked Sondra if she could let him go into the room and not follow him. She wanted to know how long he would be there. I thought that was a good question and asked him how long he needed. He laughed and said, "A day." I asked if he needed that long, and he said, "no"; he was only joking. I wondered how long he thought he needed in order to cool off. He said, "Just a little while." Since his response was vague, I asked for it in minutes. He thought he needed 5 minutes. I questioned whether he could cool down in 5 minutes, and he agreed that maybe it was too short, and settled on 20 minutes. I asked Sondra if she could let him stay in the room undisturbed for 20 minutes. She said she was glad to have him leave when he was that angry; she thought he could stay even longer. Since John decided on 20 minutes, I said we should leave it at that.

The next thing that needed deciding was which room. They both agreed that the living room was best; it had a door that

---

Anytime I feel myself getting angry, I agree to:

1. Tell Sondra that I'm too angry to continue the discussion.

2. I will lock myself in the living room for 20 minutes.

3. I will tell myself to calm down and that hitting Sondra isn't worth it. I don't want to lose control.

Sondra agrees to:

1. Let me go into the living room when I need to control my anger.

2. Not protest my leaving.

3. Not follow me into the living room.

We both agree to drop the subject which led to anger, as it is a hot topic. We will not talk about it again until the session.

_____   _____
John's Signature   Sondra's Signature

_____   _____
Worker's Signature   Date

Exhibit 6-1   *Sample Contract for Batterers*

could be closed. John originally said the bedroom, but Sondra objected: what if the fight was in the middle of the night?

John was instructed that after he locked himself in the living room, he was to tell himself to calm down, hitting her was not worth it, and he did not want to lose control. Sondra was instructed to let him go into the living room, not protest, and not follow him. Either John or Sondra could suggest that he go to the living room. If Sondra became afraid of his anger or perceived that it would escalate, she could ask him to go into the living room. If John felt himself getting angry, he would tell Sondra he had to go into the living room. After 20 minutes, he would come out. They chose not to talk again about the issue that provoked the anger and save it for the session. John could

Anytime John gets angry, I will:

1. Allow him to go into the living room.

2. Not protest his leaving.

3. Not follow him into the living room.

John agrees to:

1. Tell me when he's getting too angry to continue the discussion.

2. Lock himself in the living room for 20 minutes.

3. Tell himself to calm down and that hitting me isn't worth it. He doesn't want to lose control.

We both agree to drop the subject which led to anger, as it is a hot topic. We will not talk about it again until the session.

John's Signature	Sondra's Signature
Worker's Signature	Date

Exhibit 6-2   *Sample Contract for Battered Women*

go into the living room as often as either he or Sondra thought he should. Since John was not aware of any signals to his anger, anytime he felt angry, he would follow the agreement (contract).

I wrote down the contract and asked each of them to repeat what was agreed to. Neither could repeat it exactly, and we went over it three times until they could. They laughed at their "poor memories." Both were given a copy of the contract, and I also kept one. I told them to put the contract in a visible place. Sondra wanted hers on the refrigerator door. She suggested he tape his to the side of the television set in the living room. He agreed. I told them that I would be asking them how the week went in the next session and whether they used the contract.

It was no surprise that in the next session, Sondra and John had a critical hot topic to discuss and were avoiding discussing whether they had used the contract between sessions. They had not. A couple unconsciously colluding to sabotage efforts at changing the homeostatic system is to be expected.

The worker who recognizes the collusive efforts can circumvent them by continuing the movement toward change. Sticking to the focus on the use of the contract, which is a method of changing the violent pattern, fosters change attempts. It is natural for practitioners to want to deal with the volatile topic first, influenced by the couples' expressed need to do so and thus avoid the focus on the use of the contract. But if the use of the contract is given priority, it will be easier to circumvent collusion if it exists.

The simplest method is to table other issues until the contract discussion is concluded. A second method is to watch the clock and leave at least 30 minutes to discuss the contract, allowing the couple to discuss their agenda first (the hot topic). With Sondra and John, I asked them to table the hot topic until we discussed whether they had reason to use the contract during the week and whether they followed it. They had reason to use the contract, but they had not.

Sondra and John came early. At the appointment time, they rushed in, with Sondra starting to speak even before taking off her coat. She said there was something urgent that came up yesterday and she could hardly wait to see me. John agreed, saying it was really important. They both thought it would have been too hot for them to handle themselves if they got into it alone, so they waited for me. I said that it was good they tabled a hot topic, but I first wanted to find out whether they had reason to use the contract, and we would get into the hot issue after that. Both were silent. I asked what the silence was about. Slowly Sondra admitted that they did have a fight during the week, although there was no violence. She looked self-consciously at John and then at me. I asked what happened. Speaking quickly, she told me. John had his head down the entire time Sondra was talking, and he was silent. Sondra said that John was going to get mad all over again, she could tell. John retaliated that if she would just quit her mouthing off, he would not have to get mad.

I interrupted and said I wanted to know if that night they had followed the contract. There was silence followed by additional information about the fight. I asked my question again. John said they sort of forgot about it; they were too busy arguing. I commented that this is precisely when they are to remember to use the contract. Again, I had each of them recite the content, which they were able to do accurately the first time, and reminded them that I would be asking about it the following session.

Viewing a pattern as systemic with sequences that are repetitive and cyclical, such as Sondra and John's fighting pattern, and relearning and breaking of old patterns requires repetition and consistency by the practitioner. It may be necessary to repeat many times the instructions and procedures concerning the use of the contract. Initially, helping the couple to have conflicts that do not get out of control through the use of the contract might and usually does take up a major part of the sessions. After that, volatile topics need resolving lest they become repetitive sources of conflict. Focusing on these topics will take up the remainder of the session.

The discussion of contracts and the focus on volatile topics for resolution are also vehicles for improving couple interaction. Through their focus, couples learn good communication skills, such as saying what they really mean and feel rather than using defensive language. They learn to listen and understand the other, learn skills of empathy and sympathy, and communicate direct expressions of wants and needs. In short, the couples need to learn how to develop a mature love relationship with mutuality and reciprocity.

Jessica and Oscar said that they had to talk about the scuba diving issue. They had tried three times at home and always wound up arguing and having to use the contract. The counselor asked them to tell her the details.

Jessica said that Oscar went out and bought her equipment. She turned to him and said, "I appreciate your doing it, but it wasn't what I wanted." Oscar said defensively that there was nothing wrong with what he bought. She was not as advanced as he and what he bought was state of the art on her level. She said that the diving suit had a stain on it. He replied that it was in a place where it was not noticeable. They were always short of money, he noted, and he found a way to get her state-of-the-art equipment at a discount and now she was complaining. The salesman took 20 percent off the list price because of the stain. He said to the counselor, "First she complains about that I have state-of-the-art equipment and she doesn't. Then I buy it for her, and she complains about that too." He turned to her angrily: "I can never do anything right for you. All you do is bitch and complain. I don't know why we're still married." She retaliated: "Maybe we are better off divorcing."

The counselor asked Jessica what exactly were her objections to the equipment. She asked Oscar to listen to Jessica. Jessica started to talk to Oscar, who answered her. The counselor directed Jessica to talk to the counselor, not to Oscar, and she directed Oscar to listen and not respond. Jessica tearfully said that she knew the stain was there and it could be seen, which made her feel shabby, and that once again, she could get only second best. She thought the color of the suit was ugly, and Oscar knew that how something looked was important to her. The flippers were not the brand or style that she wanted either. She appreciated Oscar's gesture, but he had not gotten her what she wanted. The counselor asked how that made her feel. She said hurt and disappointed. It was a letdown when she opened the package because she thought that Oscar had really understood her needs, only to find out he did not.

The counselor asked Oscar how he felt about Jessica's reaction. He said he was angry. The counselor asked what else he felt beside anger. He felt criticized. And how did that make him feel? Oscar could not answer, and the counselor wondered if he was hurt. He said he was. He tried to do something nice for Jessica, and look where it got him.

The counselor pointed out that both felt hurt by the other. When questioned, neither realized the other felt the same way. The realization was a source of bonding. The counselor went further, however. She asked Oscar how long they had been married. He said 9 years. The counselor multiplied 365 days by 9 years and said that came to 3,285 days. She asked Oscar whether in the 3,285 days that he was married to Jessica, he did not know that she was discriminating about color, style, and how things looked. The worker turned to Jessica and said that she did not understand, knowing Oscar as long as she did, that he paid no attention to how things looked, thus pointing out the set-up involved and how the couple colluded to maintain their pattern of dissatisfaction with the other and not getting their needs met.

This example clearly demonstrates how resolving a volatile issue brings the system into focus. Through the counselor's efforts, the topics were dealt with, teaching communication skills of expressing hurt and disappointment were addressed, as well as identifying a systemic pattern. Of note, the counselor directed Jessica to talk to her (the counselor), not Oscar. It is common practice in family treatment to direct couples to talk to one another. But in couples where violence is present, the partners should be discouraged from talking to one another because there is not sufficient control to do this successfully. The control must be in the hands of the practitioner. In an attempt to maintain control, the couple is instructed to talk directly to the worker, with one member talking while the other listens. As treatment progresses and violence is under control, talking to one another becomes appropriate and therapeutic.

Over time, the use of the contract to stop the pattern of violence will become automatic, and couples will be able to resolve more issues independent of the sessions as their communication skills improve and their interactive patterns become more constructive. The remainder of the therapy time is spent in sustaining gains made and focusing on the marital relationship to repair the damage that was done to their relationship as a result of the history of violence.

With these methods, the violence is usually eliminated in four to six months. Couples need to remain in treatment at least one year, however, for the marital relationship to become sufficiently repaired. Some couples may choose to terminate treatment after the battering is eliminated, but they should be encouraged to remain long enough to work on other issues.

Homework Assignments

Between sessions, couples are given homework assignments. For example, couples who avoid discussions for fear of violence might be assigned a listening and talking exercise; a certain number of times a week for a specified time, each is to tell the other how the day went.

The other only listens, and they never discuss the content again. For clients who are disappointed in their partner, each might be assigned to make up a list of characteristics of their ideal partner, a list of characteristics of their actual partner, and match it. The assignment is done individually in private, and they read it to one another in the session. The results are discussed with the practitioner concerning how close the actual and the ideal are. For individuals disappointed in themselves, each makes a list of how he or she would like to be in life and in the relationship.

The same technique concerning clients' understanding of the contract is employed when issuing homework: it is written down, each repeats what the assignment is, and assignments have a due date—usually the following week.

Assignments develop out of the session content and deal with something needing practice or thinking about. They are progressive, reflecting the couple's changes. An assignment can be something the couple does together or individually. The practitioner's role is to determine whether the assignment was done and what the outcome was. The worker directs the couple to repeat orally the assignment or assigns a new one. Homework provides continuity between sessions, gives couples time to work on something important to effective treatment, infiltrates the existing system, and keeps the treatment alive between sessions.

When couples carry out assignments successfully, their positive efforts need to be acknowledged by the practitioner, just as failures are acknowledged by what we call focusing on problems, which makes up most of therapy sessions' content. In general, therapy focuses on pathology. People come in and talk about their problems. When it is possible, successes should be emphasized, drawn out, and given focus beyond a passing statement. Practitioners inquire about the success, comment on it, and mark it. When clients are behaving in a healthy fashion, that needs recognition as well; it is reinforcing and keeps hope alive. Further, I believe that people change more from a positive context than from a negative one.

MULTIPLE COUPLES GROUPS

Multiple couples groups offer the advantages of group as well as the capability of developing a 24-hour self-help hot line at no extra cost in situations where a hot line is not part of the services provided. Groups should last between 1 ½ and 2 hours a week, with the hot line used clinically to augment treatment.

Group Structure

Groups develop peer group pressure to conform or change in situations that would alienate the client if stated by the leader, provide peer group support, allow battering to be discussed openly with peers, break through isolation and denial, challenge myths, allow for people to be accepted for who they are, and provide for resource sharing. There should be a minimum of two workers staffing the group, preferably a male-female team to model an appropriate partnership; if the group is particularly difficult, a worker should be added.

The main goal of the group is the elimination of violence, and the violence-eliminating techniques described for conjoint treatment are applied. This is primarily a task-oriented, problem-solving group. It is expected that the group will last one year. Although the violence will stop before a year's time if the violence-eliminating strategies are applied diligently and consistently, the remainder of the time is used to sustain gains made in treatment in order for gains to become internalized and to focus on marital issues other than battering. The group is structured in the following way:

Step 1. Begin promptly. Beginning on time provides an external structure for people who lack some internal structure.

Step 2. The leaders note who is absent from the group and the reason for the absence if they know the reason. Otherwise, the group members are asked if they have been informed by the absent members as to the reason. There needs to be consistency about the rule that everyone attend every session to guard against a high dropout rate. Focusing on the absences conveys the message that attendance is important and develops peer group pressure to attend.

Step 3. The leaders ask how the group feels about the members' absence, and the empty chairs are left in place during the meeting.

Group members need to talk about how they feel since they do not have positive experiences with expressing their feelings. Additional reasons to share feelings about absences relate to strategy. The topic conveys the importance of each group member's attendance by giving group time to it and reinforcing peer pressure to attend. Each member hears what is usually negative reaction by the group to an absence because the members who are present can identify with not wanting to come and came nevertheless. Leaving the empty chairs symbolizes the absence. If there are no negative feelings about absences, that needs to surface so the leaders can deal with it.

The first three steps are considered the preliminaries. Steps 4 and 5 are the heart of the meeting.

Step 4. The leaders query the group concerning the issue of violence between sessions by asking how the week went. Couples who were violence free for the week share their success with the group and are helped to explain the methods they used for controlling the violence. Couples where violence was present explain step by step, in detail, what happened.

Successful couples should have the group's attention and praise. Treatment intrinsically is focused on what went wrong. There needs to be equal time for what went right. Second, acknowledgment of success is both a learning experience and a reinforcer for everyone. The couples who were successful need to be consciously aware of their effectiveness and their control over the violence rather than think it arbitrary. Other group members need to discover what works and that success is possible.

With couples where violence persists, everyone needs to hear how control broke down and that consequences were enforced. Violence usually occurs because the contract was not followed. The group and leaders reinforce the need for following the contract. The violent couples have the responsibility for not following the contract placed on them so that they cannot deny their responsibility and control. Focusing on failure conveys the message to the other members that their responsibility for upholding contracts cannot be denied or taken lightly. Sometimes violence recurs for reasons other than failure to follow the contract; the contract may be unrealistic and needs amending, or there may be more severe pathology than can be treated by this method. The workers need to be aware of reasons for failure.

Step 5. If there is sufficient time, issues other than the violence can be raised.

Because violence is so dominant in these couples' lives, other partner issues in need of remediation rarely get focused on. Beyond the cessation of violence, these couples need to repair their relationship, improve their communication skills, and bond. Focusing on relationship issues besides violence becomes relevant and appropriate.

Certainly focusing on the elimination of the violence is the main priority and first order of business; other issues are raised only after that is achieved. It may be that in any group session, the entire focus concerns the violence.

The Self-Help Hot Line

A program hot line can be used by couples in treatment in conjunction with contracts; it becomes an integral part of the treatment plan. Between sessions, either member of the couple calls the hot line when there is concern that anger may get out of control. The hot-line worker, who has a copy of each couple's contracts, intervenes. Couples are told that their counselors will know they called the hot line and what transpired, which then is discussed in the session. When couples call the hot line, the leader reinforces their efforts, instructing them to call as often as needed.

If a self-help hot line is developed, the same methodology is employed. This time, the hot-line worker is replaced by a couple. A step-by-step guide to the organization and use of the self-help hot line follows:

1. Each week or so, a couple is on call. (The group works out a policy for the length of time for being on call.) The couple must be at their telephone number or easily reached for the duration of their on-call responsibilities. A beeper system can be used, with the beeper turned over to the next "on-call" couple.
2. A copy of each couple's contract is distributed to everyone in the group.
3. Couples are instructed to call the couples on call when needed.
4. The on-call couple follows the contract of the couple who is calling and writes up a report of the transaction, all of which will be brought to the next group for review.
5. The leaders and group review the reports with the couples involved, and the next on-call couple is chosen.

Brenda and Louis were at home watching television. It was 10:00 P.M. when their telephone rang, and Brenda answered it. The caller was Linda. She said, "Brenda, Kevin is angry. I'm worried." Brenda told her to put Kevin on the telephone and motioned to Louis to get on the extension. Brenda reached for Linda and Kevin's contract. Kevin got on the telephone readily, but he was swearing and calling Linda names as he recounted what had happened. Brenda told Kevin to calm down. He replied, "How can I with that bitch insulting me! That's abuse, too, you know!" He yelled this at Linda. Louis said, "Look buddy, I'm right here for you. Brenda too, but you have to calm down . . ." Kevin interrupted, screaming, "Me calm down! I was calm, but she provoked me," and to Linda, "Right bitch!" Louis had to get his attention. He said, "Kevin, talk to me, not Linda." Brenda coaxed him. Louis continued, "You know you promised, we all did, not to escalate. Now's the time to calm down and take that walk for a half-hour." Kevin replied, "Why the hell should I? She started it, and it's late and cold outside. Let her take a walk." To Linda he shouted, "And don't come back!" Louis said, "Listen Kevin. *You* have to take a walk. Come on. It was agreed to. I was right there. Take a walk for a half-hour. It says so in your contract."

The use of the self-help hot line not only solves the problem of the need for a hot line without additional cost but is empowering to the couples because they practice self-control techniques at a time when the focus is not on them. The workers can use it in subsequent sessions to examine issues of self-control by pointing out how good a job they did when the need for self-control was directed elsewhere and not toward them, lending evidence to the fact that they know what having self-control is about. Being on call gives couples an experience of how their violent behavior feels to others, which helps develop empathy. In trying to help the couple deescalate, they learn, for example, that the anger is overwhelming, overreactive, pervasive, frightening, and inappropriate, all of which also applies to them.

There is more and more evidence of different subtypes of batterers, some of whom can benefit from treatment. Similarly, there is a growing recognition that battered women have diverse needs and that "treatment should be based on a woman's evidenced needs rather than prevailing ideology" and that she should not have her decisions controlled by the batterer or the therapist.[8]

Careful assessment determines modality. This is particularly true when assessing for conjoint work in order to avoid the potential dangers of seeing a couple who are not ready or who are inappropriate for this method. After a careful and accurate assessment is made, treatment follows.

7

Using the Systems

In addition to clinical needs, battered women interface with other systems as well; criminal justice, medical and community resources. While these systems offer benefits to battered women, they also have limitations.

THE CRIMINAL JUSTICE SYSTEM

Whether women remain in or leave the battering relationship, they often get involved in the criminal justice system. Even if they do not, they and batterers need to be made aware of legal rights for battered women and what the criminal justice system can and cannot do. Any professional working with battered women must be knowledgeable about legal issues for the purpose of educating clients, because he or she may have to act as a client advocate, and to understand how the limitations of the criminal justice system affect clients. Legal issues are intricately involved with other issues battered women face; a worker who is not knowledgeable has only a partial picture of the client's situation.

This section examines the criminal justice system, beginning with the first step of calling the police. Laws concerning domestic disputes vary from state to state, procedures differ in different jurisdictions even within the same state, and laws change. This section provides a generic description of the law for family offenses as of February 1991. Readers are advised to check with their own local criminal justice system for laws and procedures pertaining to their geographic area.[1]

127

The legal rights of battered women are quite limited; the laws are weak and hard to enforce, her recourse is little, and systems are bogged down in bureaucratic procedures. This inadequacy can be explained as a legacy of legal inaction based on the belief that there should not be outside interference in family matters.[2] Many women become discouraged about effective protection and take no legal action or do not follow through on preliminary actions. Nevertheless, for women who have the endurance to see it through, legal action might prove effective. If taking legal action is presented to women realistically concerning what the law can and cannot do, they can make a informed choice. The practitioner can arm them with accurate expectations that may cut down on discouragement. In certain instances, information on how to use the criminal justice system in spite of its limitations may help women to follow through.

CALLING THE POLICE

During a battering episode, if possible, or immediately following violence, the police should be called. The woman does not have to have her partner arrested or press charges against him. She may be asking for protection or she wants to leave. There does not have to be a legal relationship between the battered woman and the abuser for her to call the police.

When the police arrive, they prepare a report and may arrest the batterer if there is probable cause, defined by the New York City Police Department as a combination of facts viewed through the eyes of a police officer that would lead a person of reasonable caution to believe that a crime is being or has been committed. The police should inform the woman of her legal rights and the resources available to help her as a battered woman.

Arrest

If a crime has been committed and the woman wants to press charges, the police can arrest the abuser if there is probable cause. They cannot arrest because the woman is angry at him or for a similar reason.

In some communities, the police can arrest an abuser when a crime has been committed regardless of whether the woman wants him arrested if there is probable cause. The police *must* arrest in the case of a felony and for a violation of the order of protection.

The role of the police is not to mediate violence. If a woman intends to press charges and she believes that the officer is refusing to make an arrest in the presence of probable cause, she should copy down his badge number, in his presence, and tell him that she will report him to his commanding officer. If the officer still does not make the arrest, she may be able to take the following steps:

1. Go to the police station, sign a complaint, and request arrest.
2. Attempt to see the district attorney.
3. Report the officer to the civilian complaint review board.

The practitioner can also report the officer and identify herself or himself as the woman's social worker or psychologist. If the worker is part of an agency or mental health clinic, she or he should include the affiliation as well.

It is not uncommon for the abuser to take flight when the police are called, and therefore, he is nowhere to be found for arrest. The police will search for him. If they are unable to find him, they may be called to arrest him when and if he returns.

Saving Evidence

The police may want evidence saved. They may take photographs of the injuries or save torn or bloodied clothes. If they do not, the woman needs to do these things herself. The person who takes the photographs should sign and date them. Getting medical attention, in addition to ensuring that her injuries are treated, can also serve as evidence.

The victim should not cover up the cause of her injuries. Many battered women are reluctant to get medical attention and may need persuading. And if they do seek help, they do not always reveal that the injuries were caused as a result of battering.

FILING CHARGES

A woman who decides to file charges against the abuser signs a complaint and requests that the abuser be arrested. If the abuser can be located (many flee when the police are called), he will be arrested, but unless the charges against him constitute a felony, such as getting shot or slashed, he will be released within a certain period of time. (In felony charges, criminal proceedings may begin.)

The police should inform her about orders of protection, an official court paper that orders the person named to stop harming or threatening the family or household member. It may order that the person named be removed from the home, stay away from the other person, and set stipulations for visitation rights.

All orders of protection, regardless of which court issued them, have an expiration date, which appears on the front of the order. The typical length of time they are good for is one year. The order is not renewable. The woman must have new allegations of abuse to report after expiration and file again for a new order of protection.

Orders of protection may be obtained in family court or criminal court (or the state supreme court if the woman is obtaining a divorce, separation, or annulment and wants an order of protection before the settlement or trial is final). The court a woman uses may be up to her. Going to court usually follows after the police are called but can be done even if the police have not been called.

GOING TO COURT

The protocol for obtaining an order of protection varies by state. In New York State, for example, women can obtain an order of protection in either family or criminal court if the charges against the batterer are:

1. Disorderly conduct
2. Harassment
3. Menacing
4. Reckless endangerment, such as dangling a child out of a window, putting a loaded gun to someone's head
5. Assault in the second degree (which constitutes a felony). An example is using a dangerous instrument to cause serious injury.
6. Assault in the third degree (which is a less serious assault, such as inflicting cuts that require stitches, black and blue marks, a black eye, or a swollen face).

Choosing Family or Criminal Court

Criminal court is open to anyone, but a case usually goes there if a felony has been committed. If no serious felony has been committed, the choice of court may be up to the woman.

If choice of court exists, the decision should be made on the basis of what relief the woman seeks. Family court is a civil court; while its purpose is to stop the violence, no criminal conviction will occur. Prosecution in criminal court may result in a criminal conviction and may impose punishment, although there are many dispositions in criminal court that do not involve criminal convictions or jail sentences.

Usually a woman requests an order of protection after a recent battering, but she can obtain an order for a past incident as well. The statute of limitations gives her a certain number of years from the last incident in which to file for an order of protection.

There is a protocol for obtaining her order, which varies in the two courts.

Obtaining an Order of Protection in Family Court

Step 1: Filing an Application

Because of the large number of women filing applications to obtain an order of protection, the process is time-consuming. The woman should bring something with her to occupy her time— something to read, mending, knitting, and so forth. It is best that someone watch her children, but if she must take them with her, quiet games or toys for them to play with will help them pass the time. There is a first come, first turn procedure. Women should get to court as early as possible.

When the woman's turn has come, she speaks to a clerk, who will draft a petition, the sworn statement giving the facts of the case. In filing the petition, women should state the last incident first, briefly and succinctly. If the last incident of battering was not the worst, the worst should also be included. The clerk will write as much as there is room for on the petition; it is important to be brief but also to include the most serious abuse(s) and not minimize. Women should be polite but assertive.

Filing for an order of protection is routine, but practitioners should be on call for a client in the event a complication arises—

whether it is that she has lost her nerve or her patience or does not understand or remember something. This support or intervention when she wavers may help her to carry out her intention rather than change her mind. She may be able to leave the courtroom to call for help in the process, and she should be encouraged to do so.

The clerk is not a judge and does not have to be convinced; he or she just takes the facts. Clerks will not prompt women to say more; therefore, women should be prepared to say everything they want included. They can rehearse ahead of time or write down what they want to include so they do not forget.

Violence has a traumatic effect on battered women often causing them to be shaky and not in full command of themselves. Added to that are: the effort of going to court, feelings about the wait to be seen and to be interviewed by a court officer, the retraumatization of retelling the horrible events, and the feelings she carries with her about being a battered woman, which are sometimes reinforced by others. Viewed from this perspective, it takes a great deal of strength, fortitude, and courage for women to file for orders of protection.

Women tell the clerk what they want the judge to do, which can include the following:

1. Order the batterer to stop threatening or hitting her.
2. Order the abusive person out of the house.
3. Order the batterer to stay away from her and the children.
4. Give her custody of the children.
5. Set a time and place for her husband to visit with the children.
6. Order her husband, or if not married, the father of her children, to give her support money for herself and the children.
7. Order the police to assist her to remove her belongings from the house.
8. Order the batterer to pay for her lawyer if he has money.
9. Order the batterer to pay the medical bills for treatment of the injuries caused.
10. Order custody and child support even if she is not married to the father.

It is the judge's decision to rule on the order of protection, but women should not be shy in asking for various actions, and they should state everything from this list that applies.

The clerk will ask that the petition be signed and sworn as to its truth. It should be read carefully and corrected for any mistakes. Women should seek clarification for anything not understood and ask for a copy. The clerk will file the petition and set a date for a hearing in front of a judge for the woman and batterer.

Step 2: The Summons

After the petition is drafted and filed and a court hearing date is set, various documents may be given to the woman, such as a copy of the petition and an affidavit of services. A court summons informing the batterer that he has to appear in court on a specific date may be given to the woman. The petition and summons must be served before the court date to the batterer by a friend, relative, sheriff, or process server. (The process server charges for that service.) A police officer can be asked to accompany a friend or relative. The person who gives the petition and summons to the batterer signs an affidavit of service, which is notarized and then kept by the woman, who gives it to the judge at the hearing. This affidavit is proof that the petition and summons was served to the batterer in case he does not come to court.

Often batterers are angered by receiving a summons, which can put women in further jeopardy. If a woman is worried about the batterer's reaction to receiving the summons, she can make arrangements to stay elsewhere until the court hearing or have someone in the house with her whom she knows can protect her and intervene for her. The latter is a poorer choice because it could mean a confrontation with the batterer; however, sometimes there is a person of influence whom the batterer will respond to or with whom he will not be violent when in that person's presence.

Step 3: The Court Hearing

The court hearing is held in the presence of a judge who will decide if the charges have been proved. Since the U.S. Constitution states that a person is innocent until proved guilty, both the batterer and woman are expected to be present to state their case. The case can be adjourned if the batterer fails to show up; if this happens several times and if the woman so requests, she will receive an order of protection anyway. The case may also be adjourned even if the batterer does appear but without a lawyer so he has time to get legal representation. If the batterer has legal representation, the woman should also obtain a lawyer.

Most people have no experience speaking to a judge, and the battered woman should know what to expect and how to present her case. She should be on time and make a good appearance in front of the judge by dressing neatly and presenting her story well by telling all the facts without minimizing them. She can tell how the battering affected her and her children. Recalling these events may cause her to cry, which she does not have to hide from the judge. It is natural for her to feel fearful of the batterer, which she can express to the judge. Her answers to the judge's questions should be brief and clear. She should not show anger at the judge, even if she feels it.

The woman needs to do whatever she can to bolster her case, which can include bringing witnesses, medical reports of her injuries, photographs, and evidence that she reported the assault to the police. She proceeds with her story only if the judge asks her to. If an adjournment is set, she will have to wait until the actual hearing. She should address her remarks only to the judge. She should not interact with the batterer and especially should not get angry at the batterer or fight with him no matter what he says or does. The judge has complete control on the outcome of the case, and it is important for the woman that the judge believes her. How she presents herself and her story to the judge can influence his decision.

Sometimes judges grant mutual orders of protection, usually when the batterer requests one and/or the judge feels the abuse is mutual. Women should never agree to this solution because it affects arrest procedures. When both parties claim that their order of protection was violated by the other, the police arrest both of them. Further, the woman will be viewed by the judge as abusive herself—having equal participation in the domestic violence. Women do not have to agree to a mutual order of protection in order to receive their own order.

Step 4: Receiving the Order of Protection

If the judge grants an order of protection, it will state what the batterer is ordered against doing and will be granted for a specific length of time usually one year. The judge will also probably order that the batterer receive counseling, probation, a psychiatric evaluation, or treatment in a program for substance abuse, if applicable.

Enforcement of the Order of Protection

It may be up to the woman to enforce the order of protection. If the batterer violates any part of it, the woman must inform the police, who will arrest the batterer for violation of the order. They will ask to see the order of protection, which she should have available to her.

Women need to know to which court the batterer has been taken and go to the court to file for a violation of the order of protection petition by the time the batterer is brought there. If she does not file the violation petition, the court may release the batterer because the reason he was brought to court will not be known. The police precinct or the police officer who made the arrest can provide this information.

Women should find a safe place for the order of protection (batterers sometimes tear them up) and file a copy at their local precinct. While the desk officer makes an entry in the command log, the woman can inform him or her that she may need to call them for protection, thereby making known her situation.

In some locations, police policy is to arrest the offender for the violation of the order regardless of whether the woman requests it, followed by a hearing. The outcome of the hearing can result in a jail sentence of up to six months or strict orders issued to the batterer.

Counseling Interview

Sometimes when battered women appear in court, counseling is offered for her or her partner for the purpose of helping them work out their problems. Counseling does not have to be accepted. It is completely voluntary and can be ended at any time or not accepted at all. If counseling is not an option a woman chooses, she can proceed to file for her order of protection.

Temporary Orders of Protection

When there is an emergency and the woman is in immediate danger, a temporary order of protection can be obtained until a court hearing is held and an order of protection granted. This is granted immediately without the wait for a court hearing and is effective immediately. Under these circumstances, there is immediate access to a judge, for only the judge can grant a temporary order.

A temporary order of protection is time limited. Its purpose is to provide immediate protection.

When the intake clerk is seen, she or he must be convinced that an emergency exists that calls for immediate protection. If the clerk thinks this is the case, the woman will have immediate access to the judge, who will issue the temporary order.

Bruises or wounds or photographs of them can be shown. The judge should be told how fearful the woman is, with examples of why she is so fearful, including if the children are in danger. Evidence is important; it can include torn and bloody clothes, photographs of injuries and of the home if the batterer has broken furniture, and medical records if the woman has sought medical attention.

Many battered women are reluctant to seek medical attention, but it is encouraged to ensure that injuries are treated as proof of a batterer's violence. The physician can be told how the injuries were inflicted and who inflicted them. Photographs of the injuries can be taken, signed by the doctor, dated, and placed in the patient's medical records. If a doctor does not take photographs, a friend can take them. If a woman has not obtained medical attention, it may appear to court personnel that she was not injured badly enough to warrant a temporary order of protection.

Request for a temporary order should be made as soon after the violent episode as possible. If a woman waits more than two days before going to court, the court personnel may not think that she is in imminent danger, and she may need to provide good explanations of why the delay took place, (such as being too badly hurt).

If this was the first episode of violence, the court personnel may try to convince the woman that she should not take any legal action. On the other hand, if violence has occurred repeatedly, they may think this episode was no more serious than any other. In either case, the court personnel must be convinced that the violence was severe, the woman needs the court's help, and she will return for appointments.

Obtaining an Order of Protection in Criminal Court

When an offense or crime has been attempted or committed, an order of protection may be sought in criminal court provided the woman is willing to follow through on a criminal prosecution. This may be attempted with or without police involvement.

When there is no police involvement in cases involving offenses and misdemeanors, the woman may file a criminal complaint and request a temporary order of protection. She generally sees the judge the same day. The judge may give her various documents, such as a copy of the complaint, a copy of the temporary order of protection, a summons, and an affidavit. The batterer will need to be served with the summons, which commands him to appear at a court hearing. The procedure for serving the batterer is the same as the family court procedure.

If the police are called and the batterer has committed a misdemeanor or a felony, the police can make an arrest, with the batterer usually remaining in jail until arraignment. The district attorney usually asks the court for the temporary order of protection when the batterer is arraigned. A copy may be sent to police headquarters. The district attorney's office may give or mail the temporary order of protection to the complainant.

Criminal Case Pending in Criminal Court

If the complainant goes to the district attorney's (DA) office with an arresting officer, a criminal complaint is drafted. She signs a corroborating affidavit and swears the information in the complaint is true. In some localities, she sees a member of the DA's office in person; in other localities, the corroborating affidavit is mailed to her for her signature. In each case, the corroborating affidavit must be filed in court within a certain length of time or the case may be dismissed.

In every criminal case, various dispositions are possible:

1. The case can be adjourned for six months and the woman given a six-month temporary order of protection. If there have been no further incidents reported by the woman at the conclusion of the six months, the case can be dismissed. This is called an adjournment in contemplation of dismissal (ACD).

2. A misdemeanor can be reduced to a violation, which is not considered a crime. It does not go on a criminal record and the longest sentence possible is thirty days. If the defendant pleads guilty, a final order of protection can be granted.

3. The case may be dismissed. The defendant is released, and no order of protection can be issued.

4. The defendant does not plead guilty; a trial will be held.

5. The defendant pleads guilty; he is sentenced by the judge.

It is completely up to the DA's office as to what cases are prosecuted. The disposition of the case depends on the quality of the evidence, the cooperation of the witnesses, and the sentence desired.

THE PHYSICIAN'S RESPONSE

Doctors can play a unique role in helping battered women. Since battered women often do not confide in anyone about their victimization, physicians need to alert themselves to the identifying signs of abuse, as well as what to do when abuse has been noted. Ronald Chez, an obstetrician-gynecologist experienced in treating battered women, has outlined some signs:

> The composite picture can consist of repeated, subtle, nonspecific complaints suggesting psychosomatic origins. The patient may be hesitant, embarrassed, or evasive in relating her history. Overt depression, abusive use of alcohol and medications, and a history of suicide attempts may be present. A recurrent history suggestive of being accident prone is an important clue. An overly solicitous husband or boyfriend who stays close to the woman and attempts to answer questions directed at her or, in contrast, bullies and criticizes staff are also helpful diagnostic clues. On physical examination, the type, extent and location of injuries are important discriminators. The more typical locations are the head, neck, face, and those areas of the body covered by a one-piece bathing suit. The presence of bruises with injuries at several sites and in different phases of healing, a time lag between injury and presentation, and a discrepancy between the logic of how the accident happened and the nature of the injury are all supportive of battering.[3]

Another physician adds that "injuries [typically include] bruises, lacerations, broken bones, head and dental injuries. The sites of reported injury almost universally [include] the face."[4] Additionally, psychosomatic symptoms, low back pain, weakness, headaches, dizziness and fatigue, pelvic pain, hyperventilation symptoms, symptoms relating to gastrointestinal disorders, and anxiety are signs.[5]

If any of these symptoms present themselves, the patient should be questioned directly. Dr. Chez suggests that the patient should be asked, "Did somebody do this to you? Did somebody cause these injuries?" He states that "the first step is to determine the patient's needs and wishes" by directly asking, "Would you like to talk about what has happened to you? . . . what would you like to do about this situation? . . . Initial decisions relate to immediate care of the physical and emotional injuries. Is hospitalization necessary to determine the extent and type of injuries? Is it safe to return home or is there excess danger? Has a death threat been made?" Questions should also relate to the children and their safety.

For women who are battered, anything can precipitate a battering, even pregnancy, although some studies report a lessening of abuse during pregnancy. Nevertheless, physicians must keep in mind that any pregnant woman in their practice may be subjected to battering. An awareness of the problem and direct questioning will result in identification of battered pregnant women.[6]

Battered women should not be forced to take any actions against their will, however. There is a difference between concerned questioning and coercion and disapproval. Chez advises, "As with other doctor-patient interactions, this is done in a supportive environment with assurance of confidentiality and privacy. A nonjudgmental attitude, a willingness to extend time to listen, and avoidance of disbelieving or discounting responses are important."[7] Further, battered women may know what is best for them in their situation. Unless a woman has someplace she can go—relatives, friends, or money for a motel—the resources available to her may be quite limited.

"Continuing outpatient therapy of battering is not usually the function of the physician," declares Chez. "An extremely effective role for most physicians is permission giving and information giving; that is, the physician identifies the existence of the problem, supports the woman in acknowledging that the problem exists, affirms that abuse is unacceptable and must stop."[8] I recommend that the woman be informed that battering is against the law and that services exist to help her. The names and telephone numbers of community services for battered women and a hot-line number are suggested resources that physicians can provide.

Some women will deny battering, and some who do seek help often do not follow through—an expected although frustrating outcome. These women need reaching out to again and again.

Although it is not required by law that battering be reported, as do cases of child abuse, legal considerations should be noted. No reports of battering can be filed without the woman's permission. If a woman reports battering, however, medical records can be subpoenaed. "The physician has the responsibility and is not liable for recording a patient's statement or medical facts or for rendering an expert, medical opinion. . . . Direct patient quotes are appropriately bracketed with the introduction 'patient states . . .' Medical opinions such as 'suspected abuse' or 'injuries suggestive of battering' do not contain legal liability."[9]

Most women who come to the hospital emergency room with injuries sustained in domestic abuse probably are not injured seriously enough to be seen immediately. At little or no cost, a private area can be set up where battered women can wait. The area should be pleasantly decorated, and coffee, tea, or broth can be available. A battered woman's advocate, such as a volunteer, could be present to calm her, share resources, and perhaps obtain a history. Providing battered women with a private, calming atmosphere is a step in the direction of humane treatment for women who have otherwise often been mistreated.

SEEKING RESOURCES

The resources that exist in the community are shelters, hotlines, counseling and advocacy services.

Shelters

There are over 1,800 shelters in the United States, Hawaii, Alaska, the Virgin Islands, and Puerto Rico that provide a safe haven for women in danger. They may also offer crisis counseling, women's and children's support groups, individual counseling for women and children, information and referral, case management, and job readiness skills. All shelters take appropriate precautions to ensure safety, such as secret locations or guards. Shelters offer a limited stay; when a woman leaves the shelter may be dependent mainly on how long she has been there. Most shelters accept children up to a certain age (this varies from shelter to shelter), although some have restrictions about the age of male children. All shelters have strict rules concerning permissible behavior, such as curfews. Some shelters have communal living and shared space, and others provide independent living arrangements. No woman is refused based on ability to pay. Most shelters, in fact, do not require payment; they recognize that regardless of a woman's financial situation, when she flees to a shelter she is virtually indigent.

Some shelters are located in a woman's locality, and others are not. In the latter case, women and children are uprooted, possibly far from their local communities. Worse, many shelters are filled to capacity and have no space available.

Shelters are a necessary and vital service for battered women, but for many women they are unsuitable; some women will not leave their home for a residence, and others cannot get in because there is no space. For some women, shelters provide salvation, and for others, demoralization. Just as different treatment options are suitable for different women, so are shelters suitable for some women but not for others. The worker must tailor all options to each woman's needs.

Hot Lines

Hot lines provide crisis intervention, information and referral, and support. They serve as a vital link between a person in need and a practitioner. The advantage they offer is that a woman does not have to leave her home in order to obtain service; there is immediate access to help, and many hot lines operate nontraditional and long hours, sometimes 24 hours a day.[10] Hot lines have a limit to offering in-depth assistance and continuous help and are not a substitute for more substantial services, such as counseling. There is no fee for using hot-line services, and a caller can remain anonymous. There is no limit on the number and frequency of calls a caller can make.

Counseling Services

Counseling services vary from short to long term, offering individual and group services to battered women and batterers. Couples and family treatment are also available.

Advocacy Services

Battered women may need help in negotiating the systems. Advocates provide the client either accompaniment or telephone advocacy. The criminal justice system seems particularly in need of negotiating, and it is common for advocates to be present and available at court. In certain localities, advocates accompany the police on domestic violence calls or are stationed in the courts to come to the aid of battered women. In other areas, telephone advocacy is available. Activities of advocates vary: they offer information, help fill out forms, and prepare the woman for expected procedures like talking to the district attorney or judge. They may help her determine her safety and precautions to take.

Even though there are legal, medical, and community resources available, they are inadequate. Many physicians are not alert to or aware of signs of battering and how to address this issue, therefore depriving a battered woman of a potential source of help. Community resources are too few in number to meet the varied needs of battered women. The Criminal Justice System is the most glaring example of this inadequacy. The laws protecting battered women are weak and hard to enforce, the protocol ineffective, and the procedures impossible to carry out in a meaningful way. In many states, for example, wife battering is not considered a criminal offense regardless of severity or frequency. Often, batterers who flee after a battering episode are not searched for by the police and even when the batterer is present, the police may not arrest. If arrested, he does not remain in jail very long and is free to live at home until the court hearing, which generally is not immediate; a delay could be as long as two weeks. During this time, if the woman was not granted a temporary order of protection, she is unprotected.

Once a woman has an order of protection, she returns home to life with her abuser. Some men are enraged that she has obtained an order of protection. Others see it as a piece of paper and ignore its orders to stop the abuse. For some men, however, an order of protection acts as a deterrent. In these instances, the experience of going to court where a judge has found him guilty of the crime of battering will stop his abuse, but not many abusers are so compliant. In the event of another battering, she begins the process all over again of calling the police; the difference now is that because she has an order of protection, he will be arrested automatically for a violation of a court order. It gives one pause that the automatic arrest is on the basis of violating the order of protection, not on the basis that he has violated her body. Once arrested, he could receive up to six months in jail, but this rarely occurs. More commonly, the batterer is released shortly after the arrest. In family court, he and the woman may have to appear in court where another hearing will take place just like the one held when the order of protection was originally granted. At that meeting, the judge will decide the consequence for violating the order of protection.

Regardless of which court the order was granted in, fortitude and follow-through are essential through this tedious process. The outcome often presents a double bind for the woman: if her partner is not jailed, he goes home, and she possibly suffers continued danger; but if he is jailed, she suffers from the loss of his income. Further, any continued contact between them can result in her death. The fact that women who are bruised and beaten by their partners can find the strength to work through the system for the meager protection they receive is a wonder to marvel at.

Many women become discouraged and demoralized, feeling that the legal system does not work for them. The result often is that they do not use it. One woman beaten every 15 seconds in the United States is an awesome statistic; yet it is a conservative estimate based only on reported cases. In view of the response on behalf of battered women from the criminal justice system, it is understandable that more women are not reporting this crime, for to do so might subject them to another kind of assault.

8

The Practitioner's Needs

COUNTERTRANSFERENCE: THE THERAPIST'S STRUGGLE

Battered women are slow to take action, and most never leave their potentially murderous mates. It is easy for workers to feel frustrated with the grim realities they must face when treating these women. When working with the batterer, workers form relationships with and must develop positive feelings about people who are violent. When working with the couple, workers are directly confronted with a violent family system where someone is aggressed upon and someone the aggressor. In short, the worker faces a woman who has been injured physically and psychologically and a man who has brutalized her.

Upon contact, the therapist is immediately assaulted by the horror of this reality. Barbara Mathias comments, "Therapists struggle with both their revulsion and their denial, a feeling that this just couldn't be real."[1] But it is all too real, and the therapist treating battering cases needs to cope with and be effective in the work. Countertransference responses do not get enough attention.[2] Unless therapists are acutely aware of the feelings evoked as a result of working with battering, these feelings left unattended, can result in mistakes in treatment that can seriously hamper the work.

Countertransference "is the totality of the therapist's experience in relation to a particular client, conscious and unconscious, feelings and associations, thoughts and fantasies; it includes the therapist's feelings about the client as well as the therapist's feelings about him or herself."[3] Any aspect of the therapeutic relationship can, and inevitably does evoke countertransferential feelings, but the treat-

145

ment of battering is particularly fertile ground for the growth of countertransference. It is easy for the therapist to develop feelings about the abused partner and the batterer even before treatment begins; indeed, the terms themselves—*battering, batterer, abuse, beaten, victim*—can elicit a cadre of feelings. Some of the feelings these words conjure up are: abhorrence, avoidance, anger, fear, sympathy, empathy, the desire to rescue, and control.

Of the choices available—the abused woman, the batterer, the couple—practitioners may be more comfortable working with the battered woman individually. She appears helpless and dependent, and they are the victim. Working with the batterer, with or without his partner, is less popular. They are the violent partners, and they have committed a crime.

Although countertransference must always be wrestled with in this work, it feels potent and overwhelming with battering cases. This problem has been noted: "Working with family violence puts the therapist under special pressures . . . Those who work with violent families have to find some way to avoid being overwhelmed."[4] Battered women tug at our feelings of the need to rescue.

Jody entered my office looking like a scared doe. She was petite and thin, with enormous frightened dark brown eyes. Although she hung her head down so that her curly brown hair hid most of her face, I could still see the bandage above her eyebrow and the purplish bruises around her eye.

This description can evoke many responses in practitioners. They may identify with helplessness and powerlessness, which every human being has experienced. They may feel anger at her assailant or at her for being abused. They can feel empathy, which can foster dependency and perhaps revulsion. The batterer can evoke fear and intimidation of his aggressive tendencies, anger and hatred for his bullying and unfair display of physical force, or a secret admiration for his ability to control. What is triggered in each practitioner is totally individual, but the feelings inevitably arise.

One way of coping with uncomfortable feelings is to distance from them. When the feelings aroused by clients are discordant with therapists' professional self-image, avoidance is a reasonable out-come. In teaching a course on the treatment of battering, I asked the class to tell me what feelings were aroused by some case examples. The students resisted, responding intellectually, giving me interpretations, developing treatment plans, and so forth. When I insisted on an expression of their feelings, they conveyed anger at the batterer but noted they are not supposed to feel that way as professionals.

The feelings engendered by battering cases can result in a therapist's avoidance of feelings and lack of involvement, which can be manifested by not offering services to these clients and a lack of exploration of the presence of violence because they do not want to know. I believe what they do not want to know is what the feelings are that may get conjured up, some of which are possibly alien. Moreover, working with couples compounds countertransferential feelings.

COUPLES TREATMENT: EXACERBATING COUNTERTRANSFERENCE

Family therapy, which forms the theoretical framework for couples treatment for battering, has been used since the early 1950s. Practitioners who work as family therapists are aware of the need not to get pulled into the system and to resist formating of coalitions with various family members.[5]

Family therapy theory instructs that if the practitioner is sucked into the family system, treatment will fail because the practitioner will view the problem in the same way as the family (system) views it, resulting in a lack of change.[6] Every therapist has been or is a member of a family and can identify with someone in the family— parent, child, or sibling. It becomes easy to join the family unconsciously as one of its members, thereby losing objectivity and effectiveness. Every family therapist has experienced the difficulty of maintaining neutrality and remaining free of the family system. The struggle to do this has countertransferential implications.

The term *countertransference* is not usually applied to family therapy, since it is an analytic construct, although Clifford Sager has used it in this way.[7] It seems to me, however, that when family therapist theoreticians talk about resisting the system, this encompasses countertransference issues. A practitioner who is pulled into the system and thereby loses neutrality inevitably is identifying with one or more of the family members. Clearly, working as a family therapist involves the same need for self-awareness about use of self to resist the system as one uses in individual treatment to grapple with countertransference. While monitoring one's own feelings is a basic tenet in therapeutic treatment; the family therapist, the analytic therapist, and the psychotherapist all have to do the same thing.[8] The practitioner working with couples where violence is present has to do even more because the presence of violence is an added dimension that cannot be ignored and forces therapists to act quickly. Therapists must support the victim and yet not take sides, a difficult balancing act. One family therapist who works with battering cases notes that time is not available; the symptoms must be changed immediately. Moreover, decisions have to be made to ensure the safety of family members.[9] The presence of physical violence, with its potential for murder, cannot be denied. That element makes battered couples work different from other couples treatment. The feelings evoked in the therapist become very intense and easily can interfere with treatment.

Lisa, age 27, called saying she was battered by her live-in boyfriend, Jim, age 30. She called an agency that works with battered women and was assigned a counselor who helped her decide her options and move into her own apartment. She was interested in salvaging the relationship with Jim. Her counselor suggested she attempt couples therapy and referred them to me. Jim was willing to come for sessions.

In the first session, it was revealed that Jim never abused her; rather, when she became angry, she hit him. She nonetheless felt threatened by him, thinking one day he would hit her, although he denied he ever would.

In subsequent sessions, it became clear that unresolved issues from her past concerning violence resulted in her paranoid feelings about Jim. Her father had physically abused her mother. She had an older brother who remained uninvolved while she felt she needed to come to her mother's rescue and often did. She was identified with her mother. When she and Jim argued, it felt to her as if she was her mother and Jim was her father. A further complication was that she had been assaulted by someone she knew and had not resolved the trauma. She was terrified when she and Jim argued and saw her violence as defending herself. In spite of the fact that she admitted to doing the battering, emotionally she was being battered.

Between sessions, Lisa sometimes telephoned me in a panic,

telling me of her fear that Jim was going to become violent with her. Her voice would shake, and she felt helpless. She wanted me to rescue her and form a coalition with her against Jim. In one telephone call after a severe argument with Jim, she said that she needed a cooling-off period and did not want to see Jim for a while. She was afraid of his response and wanted to raise it at the next session.

I was seeing this couple at a time when my emotions concerning battered women as victims were very available to me, and my countertransference need to rescue was very strong. I sided with her, forming a coalition that resulted in a loss of neutrality and ultimate loss of the case. In this case, my own feelings and associations and my feelings about myself as a rescuer affected by self-monitoring. Although I became aware of my loss of neutrality, it was too late to salvage the case. This is not always what happens. Recognition of countertransference can be used in the patient's behalf if we know how to put it to use.[10]

I had been seeing Julia and Ramon for some time. Julia tended to be verbose, articulate, emotive, and mentally quick. Ramon was passive, sluggish, and had difficulty articulating except when angered. Although he was motivated to change his abusive behavior, his temperament resulted in his not working very hard. Julia often felt that she was doing the work for both of them and she felt exploited and martyred. In a session where we were reviewing the contract for monitoring his aggression, which had failed during a fight, Ramon was uninvolved, nonparticipatory, forgetful, and confused as contrasted to the involvement of myself and Julia. I spoke to him in an angry tone and recognized that my working harder than he made me angry. I discussed this, identifying with Julia's feelings and helping Ramon to see how his apathetic behavior was frustrating and provoked negative feelings in other people besides his wife, whose feelings he was able to dismiss. This was useful feedback to Ramon and affected his subsequent level of involvement.

No doubt, several factors worked in consort to achieve a positive result. The length of my relationship with this couple where the therapeutic alliance was firm was a major factor and not yet present in the case of Lisa and Jim, but certainly how I used countertransference was a critical element, which helped bring about a successful change.

There are many pitfalls to successful treatment of battering cases. The demands on the therapist found in family therapy are strong, and working with violence, with its lethal potential, quickly arouses powerful countertransference. However, through awareness, countertransference can be harnessed for productive use in the treatment, enabling practitioners to view family violence cases as a population to reach out to rather than withdraw from.

POSITIVE USE OF COUNTERTRANSFERENCE

Countertransference tells the therapist something about the client as well as something about himself or herself. My wanting to rescue Lisa helped me to understand her feelings of terror, aiding in my diagnosis of her even though she did the battering and she could not articulate why she was so afraid of Jim. Countertransference is an important diagnostic tool and provides a clue to the client's inner state and an experiential understanding of clients.[11] If it is not denied, practitioners can feel something of what clients feel.

The anger aroused in the treatment of battering helps the therapist to understand the element of anger intrinsic in the couple relationship. If the therapist can admit to these feelings, thereby not being afraid of them, the clients are helped to do the same. Admitting feelings that clients can trigger is important; there is therapeutic value in experiencing feelings that may be manifested in the client.[12] Perhaps most important, countertransference is inevitable in a therapeutic relationship because "all of the analyst's inherent humanness and humaneness are necessary to the therapeutic climate."[13] Countertransference feelings can be put to good use rather than suppressed.

Family violence treatment requires the therapist to be active, directive, and interventive. When the self is so fully involved, it is easy to be affected deeply by the therapeutic experience. If emotional feelings, both positive and negative, are an integral part of the therapeutic process and not restricted to what the client experiences, two major problems seem to present themselves: putting these feelings to positive use and avoiding being so drained by them that burnout is the result.

STRATEGIES FOR THERAPISTS

In addition to the recognition of how countertransference affects treatment and the steps to take in order to use it positively, practitioners need other strategies for preserving their energies so that they may continue to be able to approach the work with the enthusiasm needed to persevere with this stressful population.

Preventing Burnout

I treated battering cases from 1976 to 1980; at that point I was burned out. Although I supervised and trained others, it was not until 1986 that I was able to resume treating these cases. What I found of help for myself, as well as my staff when I directed a treatment program for family violence, follows.

1. The therapist needs a peer group or a supervisor where he or she can vent and review cases. The work is intensive. Having an outlet for the therapist's feelings is critical. There should be no censure of feelings, either on the part of the therapist or the supervisor. Reviewing cases spots the problem areas, reinforces the accuracy of the treatment, and gives new ideas. The support received from a peer group or supervisor is invaluable for both seasoned and less experienced practitioners.

2. A case load should not be composed solely of battering cases, which can be overwhelming. The best blend I have found is to have a mixture of cases. In addition to violent cases, I treat individuals in long-term psychotherapy, couples and families where the presenting problem is not violence, and group therapy. The combination that works is an individual decision, but a combination is urged.

3. There are times that I do not accept family violence cases in order to give myself a breather.

4. This work is not for everyone. There must be something that the practitioner can find appealing and satisfying about the work, or it can be deadly.

5. Most of all, there must be the belief that a batterer can stop battering and the situation can improve.

Strategies for Safety

It is not possible to work without feeling safe, and given the choice, no one should want to. Threatening client populations do not have to be avoided in order to maintain feelings of personal safety. Although I believe that when batterers come for treatment, they are genuinely looking for help, and harming the helper is not on their minds, violence can get out of control, and it is important to structure the environment for safety. Moreover, a safe environment contributes to feelings of personal safety.

Strategic Use of the Environment

The office design should enable an easy exit should the need present itself. The practitioner should not be blocked from the door. A telephone in easy reach with an uncomplicated method for calling for help is useful.

The batterer should sit far enough away so he cannot reach the worker without taking several steps. A desk or coffee table between client and therapist can serve as a barrier.

If the batterer is seated at all times, he cannot easily swing an arm. If he stands up, ask him to sit down or ask why he is standing and then ask him to sit down.

Strategic Use of Self

Be alert to any escalation of anger, assessing whether it is benign or potentially dangerous. Should the anger escalate to a dangerous level, the therapist must diffuse the situation. One way is to tell the batterer how his expression of anger is making you feel—for example, "The way you are expressing your anger makes it hard for me to understand you. Can you calm down? I want to understand." or "The way you are expressing your anger is making me tense. If you could calm down, I'll feel more comfortable. It will help me to listen to you." or "I can hear that you're very angry. Could you calm down? It's hard for me to really listen while you're behaving this way. I want to understand." In all three examples, honest feedback has been given that shows respect for the client and makes it clear that the therapist has his interests in mind. Sharing the effect of the anger has therapeutic value as well; it gives feedback about his behavior at a time when he is self-absorbed in his anger, and it points out that not just his partner is affected by his anger; rather, it affects others as well in a negative way. This helps develop awareness of responsibility. To share that his anger has a negative effect does not diminish the therapist's authority in any way. It is another form of self-disclosure, and it will diffuse the anger.

In my experience, these techniques are effective and ensure safety. If they fail, however, it is imperative that the practitioner not be harmed and leave, even if it means leaving the batterer in the office. Afterward, an assessment must be made as to whether this is a client you can continue to work with. If so, what has happened must be addressed and worked through the same as with any other case where the worker and client engaged in an interaction that was unsettled.

Fees

Private practitioners must charge enough, but how much is enough can be decided only by each individual. The work is difficult and has to be monetarily worthwhile. Many mental health practitioners work less for the monetary gains and more for humanitarian reasons and fail to place sufficient emphasis on monetary rewards. Practitioners treating battering stretch themselves to the limit, endure stress to their psyches, and offer a specialized service. Battering cases require crisis calls between sessions, and the rewards are slow in coming. If workers are not satisfactorily compensated, it will be hard to continue to treat this population effectively. Under uncomfortable conditions, the practitioner must try to be as comfortable as possible. Together with dealing with countertransference and strategies for safety, appropriate fees are necessary in helping to meet the practitioner's needs so that he or she can continue to meet the needs of this difficult client population.

9

Working Toward Change

Conclusionary Remarks

B attering cases have in common the element of violence, but not all clients have the same needs. This book has presented a number of modalities and techniques of treatment available to treat battered women and batterers. Practitioners can draw upon numerous tools of intervention, which better afford the opportunity to listen to women's needs and individually tailoring treatment to those needs.

This book is directed to those who work with battered women and batterers, enabling them to provide effective service where it is much needed. There needs to be continued experimentation and analysis regarding service delivery, however. Not every modality described in this book will be effective for every person. As we learn more about the needs of battered women and batterers, we may be able to offer additional effective models. If we consider that in the early 1970s little treatment was available, we have really come a long way.

Much has been left out of this book: marital rape, "one of the least discussed and researched problems in the family violence field"[1]; battering in gay and lesbian communities; battering of heterosexual men, commonly referred to as "husband abuse"; and the needs of children in violent homes. Nor did I discuss cultural and ethnic or urban and rural differences.

There is an intergenerational aspect of violence; violent men often produce children who believe that love, family, and violence are interwoven. Many children coming from violent homes become involved in abusive relationships. Without intervention, violence may continue into the next generation. Further, children from violent homes suffer from the emotional effects of witnessing parental abuse, and many are physically hurt as well. Working with the children is an accepted interventive step. This needs to be taught, described, and documented.

There needs to be documentation of treatment results. It is common for practitioners to be so involved that they have little time or energy for research, which becomes the academic purview. Without an analysis and documentation of treatment results, effectiveness may be limited due to a lack of dissemination of information. A joining of hands between treatment programs and research efforts is called for. More broadly, efforts on all fronts are vigorously needed: the acceptance of violence at a societal level must be changed, patriarchal attitudes and practices must be altered, attitudes and values concerning gender issues must be reshaped, the meaning of family needs new definition, effective laws prohibiting partner abuse must be implemented, and treatment techniques to aid battered women must be continuously developed. Efforts to eradicate battering should be synergistic because the need is so great. The estimate that in the United States one woman is beaten every 15 seconds is an alarming statistic. Until the time comes that not even one woman is beaten, it is important that advocates for battered women be heard, loud and clear, over and over again. Our voices should be silenced only when there is no longer a single woman huddled and fearful in her own home.

The field is fragmented, with a split between the professionals and members of the battered women's movement, the majority of whom view the problem as primarily a sociopolitical one. Heroic efforts have been made by this movement to raise consciousness, change attitudes, and have laws enacted that effectively address the issue. Battered women need their voice, and I hope they never cease to be vigilant, militant, and vocal, but battered women need the voice of proponents of treatment as well. Some people are opposed to certain treatment techniques for battered women, primarily conjoint couples counseling. They have been vigilant, militant, and vocal about the incorrectness of this approach for what my experience teaches me is spurious reasoning. This polarization in the field harms our advocacy efforts. It is difficult enough to work with battered women and even harder when colleagues are in opposition to one another. It is a dangerous thing when there is a dictum that only one view should prevail as correct and more troublesome when that view is verbalized with viligance and ferocity, combatively opposing differing views. Such tactics of intimidation and control replicate what we are against: men intimidating and controlling women who do not conform to the men's expectations. The results are counterproductive and hurtful, weakening our efforts. Regardless of sociopolitical or clinical orientation, the task of changing violence between partners is enormous. We need a cooperative effort from all vantage points: sociopolitically for the future but also clinically to relieve the pain in the present.

A

Information About the History of the Violence

1. Date on onset
2. Frequency and target(s) of violent behavior
3. Recurring patterns and escalation
4. Severity of injuries to others
5. Symptoms associated with violent episodes
6. History of previous diagnostic testing and imaging and where they were done (to obtain records)
7. History of other impulsive behavior such as suicidal behavior, destruction of property, reckless driving, reckless spending, sexual acting-out, fire setting, and criminal offenses
8. History of familial violence as a child (e.g., being abused as a child, other intrafamilial violence)
9. History of head injury, birth complications, serious childhood diseases, and other developmental problems
10. Past and current medical illnesses

From Tardiff, K. (ed.): "Causes of Human Violence," in *Concise Guide to Assessment & Management of Violent Patients*. Washington, D.C.: American Psychiatric Press, 1989, p. 11. Copyright 1989 American Psychiatric Press, Inc.

B

Research on Causes of Human Violence

1. INNATE FACTORS

   Partial complex seizures

   Subtle neurophysiologic dysfunction secondary to head trauma, etc.

   Increased norepinephrine and dopamine

   Decreased serotonin and impulsivity

   Genetic inheritance versus chromosomal abnormalities

   Psychosis and other psychopathology

   Alcohol and drug abuse

2. DEVELOPMENTAL FACTORS

   Physical abuse as a child

   Witnessing domestic violence

   Portrayal of violence in mass media

3. SOCIOECONOMIC FACTORS

   Subcultures

   Racial inequality

   Economic inequality

   Absolute poverty

   Marital and familial disruption

4. PHYSICAL ENVIRONMENT

   Crowding

   Heat

From Tardiff, K. (ed.): "Causes of Human Violence," in *Concise Guide to Assessment & Management of Violent Patients.* Washington, D.C.: American Psychiatric Press, 1989, p. 11. Copyright 1989 American Psychiatric Press, Inc.

Notes

CHAPTER *1*

Introduction

1. V. Goldner, P. Penn, M. Steinberg, and G. Walker. "Love and Violence: Gender Paradoxes in Volatile Attachments," *Family Process,* 29(4), December 1990, p. 357.

2. J. A. Geller, "Reaching the Battering Husband," *Social Work with Groups,* 6(1), Spring 1978, pp. 27–37.

3. L. H. Pelton, "Ideology, Terminology, and the Politics of Family Violence," *Readings,* 6(3), September 1991, pp. 12–17; R. Geffner and A. Rosenbaum, "Characteristics and Treatment of Batterers," *Behavioral Sciences and the Law,* 8(2), Spring 1990, pp. 131–140.

4. G. Margolin, L. G. Sipner, and L. Gleberman. "Wife Battering," in *The Handbook of Family Violence,* ed. V. Van Hasselt, R. L. Morrison, A. S. Bellack, M. M. Hersen, (New York: Plenum Press, 1988), pp. 89–117.

5. R. A. Stordeur and R. Stille, *Ending Men's Violence Against Their Partners* (Newbury Park, Calif.: SAGE Publications, 1989).

CHAPTER *2*

Why Do They Stay? Why Don't They Tell?

1. M. S. Straus, G. J. Gelles, and S. K. Steinmetz, *Behind Closed Doors: Violence in the American Family* (Garden City, N.Y.: Doubleday/Anchor, 1980).

2. Federal Bureau of Investigation, *Uniform Crime Reports* (Washington, D.C.: U.S. Government Printing Office, 1982); *Network News,* September–October 1987.

3. E. Stark, and A. Flitcraft, "Violence Among Intimates. An Epidemiological Review," in *Handbook of Family Violence,* ed. V. Van Hanselt, R.

L. Morrison, A. S. Bellack, and M. Hersen (New York: Plenum Press, 1988), pp. 293–317.

4. Conversation with an officer in the New York City Police Department.

5. R. E. Dobash, and R. P. Dobash, *Violence against Wives: A Case against Patriarchy* (New York: The Free Press, 1979).

6. E. Hilberman, "Overview: The 'Wife-Beater's Wife' Reconsidered," *American Journal of Psychiatry*, 137, November 1980, pp. 1336–1347. These findings are corroborated by Stark and Flitcraft, "Violence among Intimates."

7. R. Chez. "Woman Battering," *American Journal of Obstetrics and Gynecology*, 158(1), January 1988, pp. 1–4.

8. H. Nussbaum, "Excerpts from Her Testimony," *Newsday*, December 3, 1988, pp. 12–13.

9. H. Varenne, *Americans Together* (New York: Teachers College Press, 1977).

10. M. Symonds, "Victims of Violence: Psychological Effects and Aftereffects," *American Journal of Psychoanalysis*, 35, 1975, pp. 19–26.

11. Stark and Flitcraft, "Violence Among Intimates," p. 303.

12. L. Walker, *Terrifying Love: Why Battered Women Kill and How Society Responds* (New York: Harper & Row, 1989).

13. Symonds, "Victims of Violence."

14. E. Stark, and A. Flitcraft, "Medical Therapy as Repression: The Case of the Battered Woman," *Health and Medicine*, 1(3), Summer/Fall, 1982, pp. 29–32.

15. E. Stark, A. Flitcraft, and W. Frazier, "Medicine and Patriarchial Violence: The Social Construction of a Private Event," *International Journal of Health Services*, 9, 1979, pp. 461–493; Hilberman, "Overview"; R. Gelles, "Violence and Pregnancy: A Note on the Extent of the Problem and Needed Services," *Family Coordinator*, 24, 1975, pp. 81–86; P. Hillard, "Physical Abuse in Pregnancy." *Obstetrics and Gynecology*, 66(2), August 1985, p. 188.

16. J. Alsdurf, "Wife Abuse and the Church: The Response of Pastors," *Response*, 8(1), Winter, 1985, pp. 9–11.

17. Hilberman. "Overview."

18. S. Taylor and K. Leonard, "Alcohol and Human Physical Aggression," in *Aggression: Theoretical and Empirical Reviews*, ed. R. G. Green and E. I. Donnerstein, (New York: Academic Press, 1983), pp. 77–102.

19. Stark & Flitcraft. "Violence Among Intimates."

20. Ibid.

21. Ibid., p. 311.

22. S. Brownmiller, *Against Our Will* (New York: Simon & Schuster, 1975).

23. M. Straus and G. Hotaling, *The Social Causes of Husband-Wife Violence* (Minneapolis: University of Minnesota Press, 1980).

24. S. Steinmetz and J. Lucea, "Husband Battering," in *Handbook of Family Violence,* p. 245.

25. L. Walker, *Terrifying Love.*

26. Ibid.

27. B. F. Skinner, *Science and Human Behavior* (New York: The Free Press, 1953).

28. Hilberman, "Overview."

CHAPTER 3

Leaving: The Use of Transitional Counseling

1. Statistic obtained from the National Coalition against Domestic Violence, Washington, D.C.

2. Ginny NiCarthy, *The Ones Who Got Away* (Seattle, Washington: Seal Press, 1987), describes thirty-three battered women who left their abusers, returning time and again before ultimately leaving for good.

CHAPTER 4

Staying: Support and Survival Skills Training Groups

1. I. Yalom, *The Theory and Practice of Group Psychotherapy* (New York: Basic Books, 1985), pp. 3–4, 11, 44.

2. L. Walker, *The Battered Woman* (New York: Harper & Row, 1979).

3. M. Symonds, "Victims of Violence: Psychological Effects and Aftereffects," *American Journal of Psychoanalysis, 35, 1975, pp. 19–26.*

4. Yalom, *The Theory,* p. 227.

5. Ibid., p. 242.

6. Yalom, *ibid.*

7. K. Slaiken, *Crisis Intervention: A Handbook for Practice and Research* (Boston: Allyn & Bacon, 1984).

8. E. Rawlings and D. Carter, eds. *Psychotherapy for Women: Treatment Toward Equality* (Springfield, Ill.: Charles C. Thomas, 1977).

9. V. Goldner, R. Penn, M. Steinberg, and G. Walker, "Love and Violence: Gender Paradoxes in Volatile Attachments," *Family Process,* 29(4), December 1990, p. 357.

10. R. Gelles and M. Strauss, "Determinants of Violence in the Family: Toward a Theoretical Integration," in W. Burr, F. Hill, and I. Reiss, *Contemporary Theories About the Family* (New York: The Free Press, 1979), 1:549–581.

11. G. NiCarthy. *The Ones Who Got Away* (Seattle, Wash.: Seal Press, 1987).

12. C. Steiner, "Radical Psychiatry," in R. Corsini, ed., *Handbook of Innovative Psychotherapics* (New York: Wiley Publishers, 1981), p. 730.

CHAPTER 5

Staying: Group Treatment for Batterers

1. R. A. Stordeur and R. Stille, *Ending Men's Violence Against Their Partners* (Newbury Park, Calif.: SAGE Publications, 1989); J. Edleson and M. Syers, "The Effects of Group Treatment for Men Who Batter and 18 Month Followup Study," *Research on Social Work Practice*, 1(3), 1991, pp. 227–243; T. L. Poynter, "An Evaluation of a Group Programme for Male Perpetrators of Domestic Violence: A Followup Study," *The Australian Journal of Marriage and Family*, 12(2), July 1991, pp. 64–76; J. Beninati, "Pilot Project for Male Batterers," *Social Work With Groups* 12(2), 1989, pp. 63–64.

2. K. Tardiff, *Assessment and Management of Violent Patients* (Washington, D.C.: American Psychiatric Press, 1988).

3. Ibid.

4. J. Geller, "Conjoint Therapy: Staff Training and Treatment of the Abuser and the Abused," in *The Abusive Partner*, ed. M. Roy (New York: Van Nostrand Reinhold, 1982), pp. 198–215.

5. M. Wolfgang and F. Ferracuti, *The Subculture of Violence*, 2d ed. (Beverly Hills, Calif.: Sage 1982).

6. E. Stark and A. Flitcraft, "Violence Among Intimates. An Epidemiological Review," *The Handbook of Family Violence*, ed. V. Van Hasselt, R. L. Morrison, A. S. Bellack, M. Hersen (New York: Plenum Press, 1988), p.p. 193–317.

7. J. Geller, "Reaching the Battering Husband," *Social Work with Groups*, 1(1978), pp. 27–37.

8. I. Yalom, *The Theory and Practice of Group Psychotherapy* (New York: Basic Books, 1985).

9. Geller, "Reaching the Battering Husband."

10. Yalom, *The Theory and Practice*.

11. K. Ferraro, "An Existential Approach to Battering," in G. Hotaling, ed., *Family Abuse and Its Consequences: New Directions in Research* (Beverly Hills, Calif.: Sage, 1988), pp. 126–138.

12. L. Walker, *The Battered Woman* (New York: Harper & Row, 1979); Stordeur and Stille, *Ending Men's Violence*.

13. Walker, *The Battered Woman*.

14. J. Geller and J. Wasserstrom, "Conjoint Therapy for the Treatment of Domestic Violence," in *Battered Women and Their Families,* Albert Roberts, ed. (New York: Springer, 1984).

15. Yalom, *Theory and Practice.*

16. M. Bograd, "Holding the Line: Confronting the Abusive Partner," *Family Therapy Networker,* May–June 1986, pp. 44–47.

17. K. Tardiff, *Assessment and Management of Violent Patients.*

18. Yalom, *Theory and Practice,* p. 419.

19. Ibid.

20. P. Papp, *The Process of Change* (New York: Guilford Press, 1983); C. Madanes, *Strategic Family Therapy* (San Francisco: Jossey-Bass, 1981).

21. Yalom, *Theory and Practice.*

22. Ibid., p. 420.

23. J. Lane and T. Russell, "Second-Order Systemic Work with Violent Couples," in L. Ceasar and K. Hamberger, eds., *Treating Men Who Batter: Theory, Practice, and Programs* (New York: Springer, 1989).

CHAPTER 6

Staying: Conjoint Therapy—A Radical Approach to the
Treatment of Battering

1. L. Walker, *Terrifying Love: Why Battered Women Kill and How Society Responds* (New York: Harper & Row, 1989).

2. H. Varenne, *Americans Together* (New York: Teachers College Press, 1977), p. 193.

3. J. Geller and J. Wasserstrom, "Conjoint Therapy for the Treatment of Domestic Violence," in Albert Roberts, ed., *Battered Women and Their Families* (New York: Springer, 1984), pp. 33–48.

4. Ibid.

5. G. Margolin, L. Sibner, and L. Gleberman, "Wife Battering," in V. Van Hasselt, R. Morrison, A. Bellack, and M. Hersen, eds., *The Handbook of Family Violence* (New York: Plenum Press, 1988), pp. 89–117.

6. J. Haley, *Problem Solving Therapy* (San Francisco: Jossey-Bass, 1976). Haley's work forms the basis for this section.

7. Geller and Wasserstrom, "Conjoint Therapy."

8. M. Russell, "Wife Assault Theory, Research, and Treatment: A Literature Review," *Journal of Family Violence,* 3(3), 1988. pp. 193–208; D. Williams-White, "Self-Help and Advocacy: An Alternative Approach to Helping Battered Women," in L. Dickstein and C. Nadelson, eds., *Family Violence: Emerging Issues of a National Crisis* (Washington, D.C.: American Psychiatric Press, 1989).

CHAPTER 7

Using the Systems

1. The information presented in this section was obtained from interviews with members of the New York City Police Department, the Domestic Violence Unit of the District Attorney's Office, a criminal justice attorney specializing in battered women, and the New York City Department of Probation. The literature drawn upon was obtained primarily from M. Fields and E. Lehman, *Handbook for Abused Women* (New York: New York State Department of Social Services, 1989).

2. P. Micklow, "Domestic Abuse: The Pariah of the Legal System," in V. Van Hasselt, R. Morrison, A. Bellack, and M. Hersen, eds., *Handbook of Family Violence* (New York: Plenum Press, 1988), pp. 407–431.

3. R. Chez, "Woman Battering," *American Journal of Obstetrics and Gynecology*, 158(1), January 1988, p. 1.

4. P. Hillard, "Physical Abuse in Pregnancy," *American Journal of Obstetrics and Gynecology*, 66, 1985, p. 187.

5. R. Chez, "Woman Battering"; E. Hilberman, "Overview: The Wife-Beater's Wife Reconsidered," *American Journal of Psychiatry*, 137(11), November 1980, pp. 1136–1347; E. Hilberman, "Sixty Battered Women," *Victimology*, 2(460), 1977–1978; R. Gelles, "Violence and Pregnancy: A Note on the Extent of the Problem and Needed Services," *Family Coordinator*, 24(81), 1975.

6. Hillard, "Physical Abuse."

7. Chez, "Women Battering," p. 2.

8. Ibid.

9. Ibid., p. 3.

10. D. Stein and M. Lambert, "Telephone Counseling and Crisis Intervention: A Review," *American Journal of Community Psychology*, 12(1), 1984, pp. 101–126.

CHAPTER 8

The Practitioner's Needs

1. B. Mathias, "Lifting the Shade of Family Violence," *Family Therapy Networker*, 10(4), May–June 1986, p. 22.

2. M. Geddes and A. Pajic, "A Multidimensional Typology of Countertransference Responses," *Clinical Social Work Journal*, 18 (3), Fall 1990, pp. 257–272.

3. E. Grayer and P. Sax, "A Model for the Diagnostic and Therapeutic Use of Countertransference," *Clinical Social Work Journal*, 14(4), Winter 1986, p. 298.

4. Mathias, "Lifting the Shade," p. 24.

5. J. Haley, *Problem-Solving Therapy* (San Francisco: Jossey-Bass, 1976).

6. V. Satir, *Conjoint Family Therapy* (Palo Alto, Calif.: Science and Behavior Books, 1967).

7. C. Sager, *Marriage Contracts and Couples Therapy* (New York: Brunner/Mazel, 1976).

8. G. and R. Blanck, *Ego Psychology II* (New York: Columbia University Press, 1979).

9. Mathias, "Lifting the Shade."

10. G. and R. Blanck, *Ego Psychology II.*

11. O. Kernberg, *Object Relations Theory and Clinical Psychoanalysis* (New York: Jason Aronson), pp. 179–180; Grayer and Sax, "A Model," p. 305.

12. H. Searles, *Countertransference and Related Subjects: Selected Papers* (New York: International Universities Press, 1979).

13. R. and R. Blanck, *Ego Psychology II,* p. 129.

CHAPTER 9

Working Toward Change

1. M. Pagelow, "Marital Rape," in V. Van Hasselt, R. Morrison, A. Bellack, and M. Herson, eds., *Handbook of Family Violence* (New York: Plenum Press, 1988), p. 208.

References

ALSDURF, J. "Wife Abuse and the Church: The Response of Pastors." *Response,* 8(1), pp. 9–11.

BENINATI, J. "Pilot Project for Male Batterers." *Social Work With Groups,* 12(2), 1989, pp. 63–74.

BERSANI, C., AND CHEN, H. J. "Sociological Perspective in Family Violence." In V. Van Hasselt, R. L. Morrison, A. Bellack, and M. Hersen, eds., *The Handbook of Family Violence.* New York: Plenum Press, 1988, pp. 55–84.

BLANCK, G., AND R. *Ego Psychology II.* New York: Columbia University Press, 1979.

BOGRAD, M. "Holding the Line: Confronting the Abusive Partner." *Family Therapy Networker,* May–June 1986, pp. 44–47.

BROWNMILLER, S. *Against Our Will.* New York: Simon & Schuster, 1975.

CHEZ, R. "Women Battering." *American Journal of Obstetrics and Gynecology,* 158(1), January 1988, pp. 1–4.

COLSON, D., ALLEN, J., COYNE, L., AND DEXTER, N. "An Anatomy of Countertransference: Staff Relations to Difficult Psychiatric Hospital Patients." *Hospital and Community Psychiatry,* 37(9), September 1986, pp. 923–928.

Diagnostic and Statistical Manual of Mental Disorders, 3d ed. rev. Washington, D.C.: American Psychiatric Press, 1980.

DOBASH, R. E., AND DOBASH, R. P. *Violence Against Wives: A Case Against Patriarchy.* New York: The Free Press, 1979.

EDLESON, J., AND SYERS, M. "The Effects of Group Treatment for Men Who Batter: An Eighteen Month Follow-up Study." *Research on Social Work Practice,* 1(3), 1991, pp. 227–243.

FEDERAL BUREAU OF INVESTIGATION. *Uniform Crime Reports.* Washington, D.C.: U.S. Government Printing Office, 1982.

FERRARO, K. "An Existential Approach to Battering." In G. Hotaling, ed., *Family Abuse and Its Consequences: New Directions in Research.* Beverly Hills, Calif.: Sage, 1988.

171

FIELDS, M., AND LEHMAN, E. *Handbook for Abused Women*. New York: New York State Department of Social Services, 1989.

GEDDES, M., AND PAJIC, A. "A Multidimensional Typology of Countertransference Responses." *Clinical Social Work Journal*, 18(3), Fall 1990, pp. 257–272.

GEFFNER, R., AND ROSENBAUM, A. "Characteristics and Treatment of Batterers." *Behavioral Sciences and the Law*, 8(2), Spring 1990, pp. 131–140.

GELLER, J. "Reaching the Battering Husband." *Social Work with Groups*, 6 (1), Spring 1978, pp. 27–37.

———. "Conjoint Therapy: Staff Training and Treatment of the Abuser and the Abused." In M. Roy, ed., *The Abusive Partner*, pp. 198–215. New York: Van Nostrand Reinhold, 1982.

GELLER, J., AND WASSERSTROM, J. "Conjoint Therapy for the Treatment of Domestic Violence." In Albert Roberts, ed, *Battered Women and Their Families*. New York: Springer, 1984.

GELLES, R. "Violence and Pregnancy: A Note on the Extent of the Problem and Needed Services." *Family Coordinator*, 24, 1975, pp. 81–86.

GELLES, R., AND STRAUS, M. "Determinants of Violence in the Family: Toward a Theoretical Integration." In W. Burr, F. Hill, and I. Reiss, eds., *Contemporary Theories About the Family*, 549–581. New York: The Free Press. 1979.

GOLDNER, V., PENN, I., STEINBERG, M., AND WALKER, G. "Love and Violence: Gender Paradoxes in Volatile Attachments." *Family Process*, 29 (4), 1990.

GRAYER, E., AND SAX, P. "A Model for the Diagnostic and Therapeutic Use of Countertransference." *Clinical Social Work Journal*, 14(4), Winter 1986.

HALEY, J. *Problem Solving Therapy*. San Francisco: Jossey-Bass, 1976.

HILBERMAN, E. "Sixty Battered Women." *Victimology*, 2, 1977–1978.

———. "Overview: The 'Wife-Beater's Wife' Reconsidered." *American Journal of Psychiatry*, 137, November 1980, pp. 1336–1347.

HILLARD, P. "Physical Abuse in Pregnancy." *Obstetrics and Gynecology*, 66(2), August 1985.

KERNBERG, O. *Object Relations Theory and Clinical Psychoanalysis*. New York: Jason Aronson, 1979.

LANE, G., AND RUSSELL, T. "Second-Order Systematic Work with Violent Couples." In L. Ceasar, and K. Hamberger, eds., *Treating Men Who Batter: Theory, Practice, and Programs*. New York: Springer, 1989.

MADANES, C. *Strategic Family Therapy*, San Francisco: Jossey-Bass, 1981.

MARGOLIN, G., SIBNER, L. G., AND GLEBERMAN, L., "Wife Battering." In V. Van Hasselt, R. L. Morrison, A. S. Bellack, and M. Hersen, eds., *The Handbook of Family Violence*. New York: Plenum Press, 1988.

MATHIAS, B. "Lifting the Shade of Family Violence." *Family Therapy Networker,* 10(4), May–June 1986.

MICKLOW, P. "Domestic Abuse: The Pariah of the Legal System." In V. Van Hasselt, R. L. Morrison, A. S. Bellack, and M. Hersen, eds., *The Handbook of Family Violence.* New York: Plenum Press, 1988.

NICARTHY, GINNY. *The Ones Who Got Away.* Seattle, Wash.: Seal Press, 1987.

Network News. September–October 1987.

NUSSBAUM, HEDDA. "Excerpts from Her Testimony." *Newsday,* December 3, 1988, pp. 12–13.

PAGELOW, M. "Marital Rape." In V. Van Hasselt, R. L. Morrison, A. S. Bellack, and M. Hersen, eds., *The Handbook of Family Violence.* New York: Plenum Press, 1988.

PAPP, P. *The Process of Change.* New York: Guilford Press, 1983.

PELTON, L. H. "Ideology, Terminology and the Politics of Family Violence." *Readings,* 6(3), September 1991, pp. 12–17

POYNTER, T. L. "An Evaluation of a Group Programme for Male Perpetrators of Domestic Violence: A Follow-up Study." *Australian Journal of Marriage and Family,* 12(2), July 1991, pp. 64–76.

RABINER, C. J. "Countertransference Issues in Inpatient Psychiatry." *Psychiatric Journal of the University of Ottawa.* 11(3), September 1986. pp. 156–161.

RAWLINGS, E., AND CARTER, D., EDS. *Psychotherapy for Women: Treatment Toward Equality.* Springfield, Ill.: Charles C. Thomas, 1977.

ROBBINS, S., AND JOLKEVAKI, M. "Managing Countertransference Feelings: An Interactional Model Using Awareness of Feelings and Theoretical Framework." *Journal of Counseling Psychology,* 34(3), July 1987, pp. 276–282.

SAGER, C. *Marriage Contracts and Couples Therapy.* New York: Brunner/ Mazel, 1976.

SATIR, V. *Conjoint Family Therapy.* Palo Alto, Calif.: Science and Behavior Books, 1967.

SCHECTER, S. *Guidelines for Mental Health Practitioners in Domestic Violence Cases.* Washington, D.C.: National Coalition Against Domestic Violence, 1987.

SEARLES, H. *Countertransference and Related Subjects: Selected Papers.* New York: International Universities Press, 1979.

SKINNER, B. F. *Science and Human Behavior.* New York: The Free Press, 1953.

SLAIKEN, K. *Crisis Intervention: A Handbook for Practice and Research.* Boston: Allyn & Bacon. 1984.

STARK, E., AND FLITCRAFT, A. "Violence Among Intimates: An Epidemiological Review." In V. Van Hasselt, R. L. Morrison, A. S. Bellack, and M.

Hersen, eds., *The Handbook of Family Violence.* New York: Plenum Press, 1988.

―――. "Medical Therapy as Repression: The Case of the Battered Woman." *Health and Medicine, 1(3),* Summer/Fall 1982, pp. 29–32.

STARK, E., FLITCRAFT, A., AND FRAZIER, W. "Medicine and Patriarchal Violence: The Social Construction of a Private Event." *International Journal of Health Services,* 9, 1979, pp. 461–493.

STEIN, D., AND LAMBERT, M. "Telephone Counseling and Crisis Intervention: A Review." *American Journal of Community Psychology,* 12(1), 1984, pp. 101–126.

STEINER, C. "Radical Psychiatry." In R. Corsini, ed., *Handbook of Innovative Psychotherapies.* New York: Wiley, 1981.

STEINMETZ, S., AND LUCEA, J. "Husband Battering." In V. Van Hasselt, R. L. Morrison, A. S. Bellack, and M. Hersen, eds., *The Handbook of Family Violence.* New York: Plenum Press, 1988.

STORDEUR, R. A., AND STILLE, R. *Ending Men's Violence Against Their Partners.* Newbury Park, Calif.: SAGE, 1989.

STRAUS, M. S., GELLES, G. J., AND STEINMETZ, S. K. *Behind Closed Doors: Violence in the American Family.* Garden City, N.Y.: Doubleday/Anchor, 1980.

STRAUS, M., AND HOTALING, G. *The Social Causes of Husband-Wife Violence.* Minnesota: University of Minnesota Press, 1980.

SYMONDS, M. "Victims of Violence: Psychological Effects and Aftereffects." *American Journal of Psychoanalysis,* 35, 1975, pp. 19–26.

TARDIFF, K. *Assessment and Management of Violent Patients.* Washington, D.C.: American Psychiatric Press, 1988.

TAYLOR, S., AND LEONARD, K. "Alcohol and Human Physical Aggression. In R. G. Green, E. I. Donnerstein, eds., *Aggression: Theoretical and Empirical Reviews.* New York: Academic Press, 1983.

WALKER, L. *The Battered Woman.* New York: Harper & Row, 1979.

―――. *Terrifying Love: Why Battered Women Kill and How Society Responds.* New York: Harper & Row, 1989.

WILLIAMS-WHITE, D. "Self-Help and Advocacy: An Alternative Approach to Helping Battered Women." In L. Dickstein and C. Nadelson, eds., *Family Violence: Emerging Issues of a National Crisis.* Washington, D.C.: American Psychiatric Press, 1989.

WOLFGANG, M., AND FERRACUTI, F. *The Subculture of Violence.* 2d ed. Beverly Hills, Calif.: Sage, 1982.

VARENNE, H. *Americans Together.* New York: Teachers College Press, 1977.

YALOM, I. *Theory and Practice of Group Psychotherapy.* New York: Basic Books, 1985.

Index

175